A GERMAN IN THE YANKEE FATHERLAND

Lt. Henry A. Kircher in the summer of 1863.

A German
in the
Yankee Fatherland

The Civil War Letters of Henry A. Kircher

edited by

Earl J. Hess

For all the brave strong men—devoted, hardy men—who've forward sprung in freedom's help, all years, all lands,
For braver, stronger, more devoted men—

Thanks—joyful thanks!—a soldier's, traveler's thanks.

"Thanks in Old Age"
Walt Whitman

The Kent State University Press

The letters appearing in this book are from the Engelmann-Kircher Papers, Illinois State Historical Library, Springfield, Illinois.

The photos on pp. 70 and 142 are reproduced by permission of the Massachusetts Commandery, Military Order of the Loyal Legion and the U.S. Army Military History Institute. The remaining photos and the reproductions of the Kircher letters are used by permission of the Illinois State Historical Library.

Library of Congress Cataloging in Publication Data

Kircher, Henry A. (Henry Adolph), 1841-
    A German in the Yankee fatherland.

    Most of the letters were translated from German.
    Bibliography: p.
    Includes index.
    1. Kircher, Henry A. (Henry Adolph), 1841-   . 2. United States—History—Civil War, 1861-1865—Personal narratives. 3. United States—History—Civil War, 1861-1865—Participation, German American. 4. United States. Army. Illinois Infantry Regiment, 9th (1861-1865)—Biography. 5. Mississippi River Valley—History—Civil War, 1861-1865—Campaigns. 6. United States—History—Civil War, 1861-1865—Campaigns. 7. Soldiers—Illinois—Biography. 8. German Americans—Illinois—Biography. I. Hess, Earl J. II. Title.
E601.K57   1983   973.7'81   83-11258
ISBN 0-87338-289-7

For my mother and the memory of my father

Contents

MAPS

ILLUSTRATIONS

Preface

The reasons for adding yet another book of Civil War soldier letters to the dozens that have already been published are threefold. First, as source material, these letters are superior in quality. Henry Kircher, more articulate and perceptive than most soldier-commentators, provided a useful source of information and opinion on Federal operations in the Mississippi Valley. The letters and occasional diary entries offer little upon which to base new interpretations, but they reinforce what we already know, further illuminate subjects that have been given scant attention (such as campaign life aboard river steamboats), and also thoroughly entertain us with Kircher's witty style.

Second, Kircher's ethnic heritage and upbringing made his letters special representatives of a long-ignored segment of Lincoln's army. Foreigners made up a substantial part of the Union military, but their contributions and reactions to the war were far from adequately covered by historians. Kircher was an Illinoisan by birth, but he also was a product of the German-American environment in which he was raised. Mid-nineteenth-century society drew lines around the ethnics, and in turn they drew lines of their own. Kircher's devotion to the Union coexisted with his awareness of an identity separate from "American" society. He provided a worthy example of partial ethnic assimilation. Contrary to popular belief concerning the war as a melting pot, Kircher's letters help suggest that a sense of separateness remained strong throughout the conflict.

Finally, the personal spirit evident in the letters is impressive. They record the passage of a shy young machinist into sometimes bitter maturity. It is not unusual to perceive a man's development through his war letters, but in Kircher's case we have the added advantage of seeing his war experience as an integral part of the rest of his life. The drama of his army years was no greater than the quieter, more sustained drama of his postwar civilian life, when he struggled against combat related disabilities to build a personally fulfilling life. His success is inspirational.

The Kircher letters were donated to the Illinois State Historical Library at Springfield by Theodore E. Kircher, Henry's son, in 1946. They remained in the German language, unavailable for use by most historians, until 1974, when I initiated efforts to translate them into English. The letters were written in old German script, which was dropped from common usage many decades ago, limiting the choice of translators to a relatively few who could remember or had been willing to learn that legacy of the past. I wish to thank Mr. Ernest J. Thode, Jr., who translated most of the sixty-four letters reproduced here, and Mrs. Gerda Kohnke, who worked on several of them. Unless otherwise cited, all letters used in this book can be found in the Engelmann-Kircher Collection of the Illinois State Historical Library.

An explanation of my editorial policy is especially appropriate in this case. A perfect translation from one language to another is virtually impossible. German sentence structure differs from our own and any given German word can conceivably have several English equivalents, depending on the thoughts of the author and the context in which they are written. Mr. Thode and Mrs. Kohnke are professionals. They aimed at a true, objective translation, as nearly as possible. Where necessary, I settled questions of phraseology and word selection based on what I perceived to be consistent with the general tone and style of Kircher's writing and outlook, and with that of his times. I gladly absolve my translators of all blame for any irregularities or misconstructions, and bear such mistakes on my own shoulders.

Some letters that did not reveal new, worthwhile material were not included and passages of the same quality were also excluded from letters that do appear. Everything enclosed by parentheses is original material; everything in brackets is mine. I revised punctuation and divided some excrutiatingly long paragraphs in the German letters in order to enhance comprehension.

Kircher's four diaries were written in English and serve to fill empty spaces between the letters. The discrepancies between their faulty spelling and sentence structure and the more assured style of the letters are prominent. Because he was raised in an ethnic environment, it is reasonable to assume Kircher could express himself better in German, and a misspelled German word is impossible to transcribe authentically into another language. The improvement of Kircher's English, most evident when comparing the entries of 1861 with those of late 1863, is notable.

The diary passages are quoted accurately with the minimal editing identified by brackets. Henry Goedeking's letter to Henry Kircher in chapter one, Kircher's letter to George in chapter two, and all of Albert Affleck's letters to Kircher in chapter eight were written in English. They also are reproduced exactly.

Kircher inserted English words into his German letters, sometimes in an attempt to record dialect. Those are easily recognized by their misspelling, which is true to Kircher's original. I did not identify the few English words that he gratuitously included and spelled correctly, because almost any form of identification that could be used would conflict with other usages. For example, Kircher sometimes enclosed German phrases in parentheses or quotation marks, or placed lines under them for emphasis. At any rate, the number of English words is so few and so little special significance appears to have been attached to their use that it seemed of little importance to identify all of them. The reader will also notice a discrepancy in the capitalization of "Rebel"; in Kircher's writing, its first letter is in lower case and in the narrative it is capitalized. Northern writers of the 1860s almost never capitalized the word when referring to Confederates, but writers today capitalize it almost invariably.

Besides the two translators, I wish to thank Mr. Paul Spence, formerly manuscript curator of the Illinois State Historical Library, for his aid in facilitating my initial work with the Kircher papers. The staffs of that institution, the State Historical Society of Missouri at Columbia, the Missouri Historical Society at St. Louis, the Belleville Public Library, and the Adjutant General's Office at Jefferson City, Missouri, also deserve a note of gratitude. My sister provided a place to stay during my many trips to Springfield. The original maps were sketched by myself and drawn by Jorge Faz. The staff of the Kent State University Press, particularly Director Paul H. Rohmann and Editor Laura Nagy, are recipients of my heartfelt gratitude. I owe to all others who were interested in this project a thank you: for, as Whitman put it, "sweet appreciation."

CHAPTER ONE

"Your Loyal Son"

When Abraham Lincoln called for troops on April 15, 1861, to deal with the South's secession, the citizens of Belleville, Illinois reacted enthusiastically. They gathered at the Courthouse that evening to express a community of feeling typical of many Northern towns. With the symbol of county government towering above them, the mixed German and native-born populace of the southwestern Illinois town heard speeches in both languages and adopted a proclamation that verbalized their faith in the Union. They "Resolved, That the people of old St. Clair County ought and will stand by the President, and faithfully support him in keeping the oath he has registered in Heaven, to preserve, protect and defend the Constitution of the United States, and see that the laws are faithfully executed."[1]

A few days later, 150 men followed August Mersy to Springfield. There they became Companies A and B, 9th Illinois Infantry, and committed themselves to serving the government for three months.[2] The long decades of idealogical conflict finally gave way to physical war; the long ingrained commitment to political union finally met a challenge that required action to back up rhetorical resolutions shouted into an April evening.

Nineteen-year-old Henry Adolph Kircher, a machinist by trade, might have heard those determined words at the Courthouse; he certainly was one of the young men Mersy led to the state capital. Although born in distant Beardstown, Illinois on November 10, 1841, Kircher had come to be vitally involved in the German community of St. Clair County by 1861. Both of his parents were German natives who had sought homes in western Illinois. Born in Fulda, Kur-Hessen, Joseph Kircher had studied law at Munich as a schoolmate of Gustave Koerner, a prominent immigrant citizen of Belleville. The elder Kircher settled in Beardstown after coming to the United States in 1833, and married Augusta Berchelmann, sister of the noted Belleville physician Adolphus G. Berchelmann, three years later.[3]

The Kirchers began to build a family unit of ten children that was community conscious and tightly knit.[4] After moving his family to Belleville in 1848, Joseph opened a hardware store in partnership with Henry Goedek-

---

[1] *Belleville Advocate,* Apr. 19, 1861.
[2] Ibid., Apr. 20, 1894; Mar. 10, 1911.
[3] Ibid., Jan. 10, 1873; May 4, 1888.
[4] Ibid., Jan. 5, 1900.

ing.[5] In his educated father and in Goedeking, his godfather and close friend, the young Henry Adolph discovered masculine role models that influenced his philosophy of living. Joseph became librarian of the St. Clair County Library Association, which was housed in a room above his store, in 1855. Henry Goedeking served as president of Belleville's first school board in 1847 and as mayor of the town in 1861 and 1862.[6] Both exhibited a sense of disinterested community responsibility, a family tradition the young man continued in his own life. Henry's mother also proved to be important in influencing his outlook, as is revealed in his wartime letters.

Henry's guidance and education began early. Joseph sent his son to Oakfield Academy when the boy turned twelve. Established several years before by Frederick Steines, Oakfield became one of the first German-American schools west of the Mississippi. Located near St. Louis on Steines's farm, it attracted children from St. Clair County, including the brothers Joseph and Fred Tell Ledergerber.[7] Leaving the academy with the rudiments of an education, Henry learned the machinist's trade and worked for three years before the great sectional war broke out.[8]

Belleville's response to the conflict was strongly influenced by its German population. Founded in 1814 on a site fifteen miles southeast of St. Louis, the town struggled during its first decade to keep alive. In the late 1820s, Belleville began to grow and prosper materially, helped in no small degree by the influx of German farmers and merchants who began numerically to challenge the Anglo-Saxon pioneers. Although the percentage of Germans among Belleville's 7,520 citizens in 1860 was not included in the published census returns, 43.3 percent of the county's 37,694 citizens were foreign-born. Only two other Illinois counties held comparable or higher percentages, contrasted to a state-wide proportion of 18.9 percent.[9]

The immigrant population had come to St. Clair County in two waves. Many educated, professional Germans arrived in the 1830s, and because they tried to bring a little culture to the semideveloped region, they became known as Latin Farmers. This group included Gustave Koerner, who was elected lieutenant governor of Illinois in 1852. Later, merchant Joseph Kircher cast his lot with these people. Refugees of the unsuccessful German

[5] Ibid., May 4, 1888.

[6] History of St. Clair County, Illinois (1881; reprint, Marissa, Ill., 1975), 188, 190. Alvin Louis Nebelsick, A History of Belleville (1951; reprint, Belleville, 1978), 154.

[7] William G. Bek, "The Followers of Duden," Missouri Historical Review 16, no. 1 (1921):119–27, 137, 140.

[8] Newton Bateman, ed., Historical Encyclopedia of Illinois and History of St. Clair County, vol. 2 (Chicago, 1907), 1054.

[9] Newton Bateman et al., eds., Historical Encyclopedia of Illinois and History of Evanston, vol. 1 (Chicago, 1906), 43. History of St. Clair County, 187, 188. Joseph C. G. Kennedy, Population of the United States in 1860; Compiled From the Original Returns of the Eighth Census, bk. 1 (Washington, D.C., 1864), 99, 103. Fayette County, in south-central Illinois, held the same percentage and Chicago's Cook County held 49 percent.

Missouri and Arkansas

revolutions of 1848–49 made up the second wave. Peter J. Osterhaus became the most distinguished representative of this romanticized addition to the foreign-born community.[10] Predominantly, the Germans held pro-Union and antislavery views. When Forty-Eighter August Mersy led his 150 volunteers to Springfield, most of them were fellow Germans.

---

[10] Julius Goebel, "Gustave Philipp Koerner," *Dictionary of American Biography*, ed. Dumas Malone, vol. 10 (New York, 1933), 496. C. C. Benson, "Peter Joseph Osterhaus," *Dictionary of American Biography* 14:88.

Kircher's service in the 9th Illinois proved to be a good introduction to the varied qualities of soldier life. After it organized at Springfield, the regiment proceeded to Cairo, Illinois, located at the strategic junction of the Mississippi and Ohio rivers. Mersy's Company A helped clear the regimental campground, Camp Defiance, of driftwood and stumps.[11] The captain noted that his young Sergeant Kircher adjusted well but appeared too reserved. On May 12, Mersy wrote to Joseph that "Heinrich is well and healthy and the only thing that I always have to disagree with and correct in him is that he is too *shy*. A little more audacity can't hurt. He is willing and does every duty without the slightest objection, and I hope that the shy being will disappear after the first cloud of powder."[12]

Kircher's mother and sisters Josephine and Louise kept in touch with him through the mail, contributing to the half bushel of correspondence that, according to Mersy, arrived every day for his company. The women baked sugar cookies and a silver cake in response to Kircher's call for "a little bit to eat," and Sgt. Albert Affleck of the 9th Illinois, affectionately called Bert and destined to become Kircher's closest wartime friend, carried the treats to Cairo.[13]

Kircher quickly learned while at Cairo that patriotism was intertwined with politics, a fact of military life that Mersy identified as "a curse that prevails over our entire system."[14] The young man considered advancement to an officer's commission but thought twice after discovering what it entailed.

Camp Defiance May 10, 61. Saturday

Dear Father!

Since you are usually very sparse with your praise and you were this time very liberal in your letter with it, I appreciated doubly. But to advance, at least now, will be very hard and I am convinced that you are much more satisfied with my present position than if I had a higher position under the following conditions. Especially since I have the good fortune to come from Latin-speaking people,[15] who are very sparse here. You have to be much meaner than the average German to gain his respect. However, as a Latin you have some kind of special esteem and obedience. Even if they gripe

[11] Marion Morrison, *A History of the Ninth Regiment Illinois Volunteer Infantry* (Monmouth, Ill., 1864), 10.
[12] August Mersy to Joseph Kircher, May 12, 1861.
[13] Ibid. Josephine, Augusta and Loulou to Henry Kircher, June 4, 1861. Josephine was often referred to as Joe.
[14] August Mersy to Joseph Kircher, May 12, 1861.
[15] Educated, cultured people.

in a friendly way, however, you have to tell them dirty jokes and jestures. (You must know, officers are being elected by the soldiers—Commissioned Officers [that is], the 1st and 2nd Lieutenants and the Captains. The Sergeants and Corporals, however, are being elected by the Captains.)

Besides that, you have to tell them nice things and not forget to *treat* them. And you still have to have all kinds of special merits, which unfortunately I do not possess. If you have scrutinized all those reasons you will be content with your present Sergeant as compared to an Officer, who would be ashamed to appear before your eyes again. Therefore you will probably forgive me when I go the way that seems to be the right one for me. On account of that, I will not neglect to climb up when I have the opportunity, be it by skill with weapons or through another opportunity.

How is mother? George wrote to me yesterday that she had her eternal headache again.[16] Are the others alright? I had just on the very same day as Uncle was here a boil under my left arm.[17] It hurt me so badly the next day that I couldn't wear my jacket anymore and on the following night got a bad cold. And on account of that I got a toothache and then a swollen face, but now it is better.

Our barracks are so bad that each time it rains we get completely wet, and lately this has happened very frequently. It always rains very hard, since both rivers attract thunderstorms.

Last night, an accident happened. One of the sentries, of the Tiedemannischen Company,[18] fell last night when it rained horribly, as he just started his beat. He fell down and his rifle discharged itself and hit a soldier in the guardhouse in the abdomen. Life and death are fighting, probably the latter one will win.

Tell them they shouldn't take it all too seriously and to write to me often, because otherwise there is nothing new here. We are all rather well. Greet all of them from all my heart.

Your obedient son Henry

The political maneuvering accounted for Kircher's dissatisfaction with the 9th Illinois. Well before his term of service expired, he and his Belleville friends apparently decided not to sign up when the time came for the regi-

---

16 George H. A. Kircher, Henry's younger brother.
17 Adolph Berchelmann. Kircher also referred to Henry Goedeking as Uncle but Berchelmann's visit to the 9th Illinois was verified in August Mersy to Joseph Kircher, May 12, 1861.
18 Capt. Dietrich F. Tiedemann's Company C, 9th Illinois.

ment to organize for a three-year tour of duty. His letters prompted Goedeking to offer the advice of an older, more mature mind to the young recruit.[19]

Belleville June 8, 1861

My dear Henry

It seems, that there is a screw loose somewhere in your camp; where & how I cannot find out. Your father & I have solicited therefore Mr. Scheel to go down and examine with you and others this matter.

We think that it does not look very patriotic, if you should quit the military service now, after having had the intention to serve your country in this war, and it might give cause of sneering remarks to some people here, who are hostile against you boys of superior education.

I have read all your letters, and must confess, that your reasons for returning home are very proper & nice and highly approvable, but those reasons were in existence at the time when you left here.

Now my advice is, that you should or shall not stay in Cairo or in your regiment any longer, if all your friends leave. But if all your friends or at least the most of them will enlist again during [the] war you should do it too.

There may be good causes for you all to disband, which I do not know; if so, come home. By no means enlist yourself alone.

You may state to Mr. Scheel all your privat reasons for going home or write the same to me by him.

My love to you from your

best friend Henry Goedeking

At least part of the antagonism within the 9th Illinois stemmed from ethnic differences between Germans and Americans.[20] Those bickerings proved to be the worst enemy the regiment faced during its three months of garrison duty at Camp Defiance. It saw no action during that time and when it mustered out on July 26, Kircher and his friends went home. The 9th Illinois reorganized for three years with August Mersy rising to its command in early September.[21]

Kircher set his sights on more ethnically congenial fields. Across the Mississippi in St. Louis, Peter Joseph Osterhaus also organized a regiment for three years service. Missouri lay in more immediate danger of Confeder-

---

[19] This letter was written in English.
[20] August Mersy to Henry Goedeking, May 3, 1861.
[21] *Report of the Adjutant General of the State of Illinois,* vol. 1 (Springfield, 1900), 432.

ate power than did Illinois, and the divided loyalties of its people left the state's recruit quotas only partially filled. On August 7, Kircher and a group of German Bellevillers left for St. Louis and two days later enlisted as Company A, 12th Missouri Infantry. A second group, led by Fred Tell Ledergerber, left August 8 and became Company B.[22] They formed the vital core of Osterhaus's new regiment.

Kircher certainly found a German enclave in the Union army. By September's end, the 12th Missouri nearly completed its organization and could boast a ratio of more than nine immigrants for every native-born member. Over 84 percent of those foreigners were Germans.[23] Kircher and most of the other native Americans, for all practical purposes, thought and acted like the foreign-born.

The regiment came to be dominated by Illinoisans as well as by foreigners. Although Sucker State recruits filled only two of the unit's ten companies, they ran the 12th Missouri for most of its service. Colonel Osterhaus had moved from St. Clair County to St. Louis before the war, but led the regiment only briefly in the field.[24] Lt. Col. Otto Schadt, an immigrant Missourian, commanded it a few months before giving way to Maj. Hugo Aurelius von Wangelin, a Prussian army veteran, native of Germany, and resident of Lebanon, Illinois. Wangelin led the unit for more than half its three-year service.[25] Capt. Jacob Kaercher and Lt. Joseph Ledergerber of Company A, and Capt. Fred Tell Ledergerber of Company B all rose in rank to exert Illinois influence in the 12th Missouri's administration. Kircher imitated their rise, but not, as he had feared in the 9th Illinois, at the expense of his integrity.

In contrast to the security of Cairo, central Missouri teemed with evidence of war that September. Confederate forces penetrated to the Missouri River and Federal Gen. John C. Frémont cranked his newborn army into motion to send it after them. Osterhaus's regiment left St. Louis on September 23 to steam up the Missouri. It camped at Jefferson City and settled down for a few days of waiting. Brigade command called Osterhaus immediately upon his arrival. Schadt took over the regiment and Kircher sorted through the hodgepodge of an army on the move to find time for a letter home.[26]

---

[22] Henry Kircher diary, entries for late September, 1861; diary entries hereafter cited as Diary. *Belleville Advocate,* Aug. 9, 1861. Enrolling officers recorded Kircher's physical description: 5 feet 8 inches tall, with dark hair, hazel eyes and fair complexion. Descriptive Roll, 12th Missouri Infantry, Adjutant General's Office, Jefferson City, Missouri.

[23] Earl J. Hess, "The 12th Missouri Infantry: A Socio-Military Profile of a Union Regiment," *Missouri Historical Review* 76, no. 1 (1981): 60.

[24] Benson, "Osterhaus," 88. Muster rolls, Peter J. Osterhaus service record, National Archives; National Archives hereafter cited as NA.

[25] Schadt left the regiment because of illness. Muster rolls, Otto Schadt service record, NA. *Belleville Advocate,* Mar. 2, 1883.

[26] Diary, entries for late September, 1861.

Jefferson City October 1, 1861

Dear Father!

This is the first birthday which we celebrate without being to-gether.[27] I would have liked to send you my picture but I could not because there was such confusion until now that I did not even get to write, much less have my picture taken. Besides, there was such bad and rainy weather through the whole time that I could not have done it at all. To my greatest joy, I heard some time ago that you are well again.

We are located here prettily on a high point with the front to the river and our rear protected, and near the [state] prison. We see from time to time a few of the inmates over the wall who pursue their daily work.

We will depart today seemingly by Pacific Railroad to Sedalia. There, as I have heard, the various army divisions will meet in order with united power, finally, to give a deathblow to the enemy.

As I have heard, our Colonel is no more, but is General Oster-haus; for him I am heartily happy. But we all would have preferred to have kept an able man such as he in our regiment. Col. [Gus-tave] Koerner was with us several times and greeted us in a very friendly manner and inquired about us with concern.[28]

Although my letter will be a little late, it will nevertheless be received just as friendly as if it had come in time for your birthday.

Because I cannot do it myself, accept from Mother in my stead a hearty kiss, with the wish that you may have many more birth-days even in happy times and in the circle of your whole family. The next one we will perhaps be able to celebrate together. When I will have a chance to write again I do not know. But all be heartily greeted and remain well and happy.

Your loyal son Henry Kircher

Kircher, like the 12th Missouri, started his true initiation into the Civil War after leaving Jefferson City. He and the regiment trudged behind General Frémont toward the southwest, toward Springfield, pursuing the Rebels, passing through towns whose names form a litany of their route through war. At Bolivar they "were causioned by L. Col. Schadt not to take any eatables or drink while passing through [town] being that the [inhabitants] were accused of being rather free and friendly in presenting us with poison."

---

[27] Joseph's birthdate was Sept. 29.
[28] Osterhaus remained a colonel until June, 1862. Koerner had been appointed an officer on Frémont's staff.

When he reached Springfield, he viewed the field where Frémont's body-guard had charged the Rebel rear in the only fighting of the campaign. "F[ou]nd 8 bodies of horses and 2 of mules, found also 3 large graves wher Secesh had been buried day before [,] 85 Bodies *in number*."[29]

The war had become something more than a three-month vacation at Cairo and home-baked sugar cookies. But alongside the cruel fact there was still room for youthful fancy. In the same diary entry that told of his discovery of war's effects, Kircher drew a hand pointing to: "Discovered a great many beutifull Galls, with black bright Eyes and b[l]ack hair, while passing through *Springfield*."

Wherever he went, ethnic sensitivity followed. In November, his division marched south of Springfield but turned back when higher authority decided to abandon the town. David Hunter, Frémont's successor, ordered the withdrawal for strategic reasons, but Kircher reacted to it differently. "I concluded it was a Trick of Genr H. thin[k]ing perhaps in this way to get rid of the dutch Genr [Franz Sigel] and his Sour crout stock." Sigel's men caught up with the others as they headed for winter quarters at Rolla.[30]

The harshness of the war's first winter was eased by good friends and jovial spirits. The holiday celebrations began five days before Christmas, when Kircher tasted his first beer since leaving St. Louis the previous fall. He spent "New Y night with great trouble, on account of several of our Comp. being tipsy, [who] threatened to thrash the Orderly but finally were stopped. . . . being bound to tease the orderly some way, they concluded to breake his tent . . . which they did." Kircher found more peace the next day. "Several of us in order to take revenge for new year's Night had a deasend little drunk at Lieut Affleck's Tent."[31]

Osterhaus's promotion to brigade leadership in October had created a ripple in the regimental chain of command. Schadt and Wangelin had moved up and Jacob Kaercher had become acting major. Affleck had taken over Company A and Kircher became its acting second lieutenant on January 15, 1862.[32] That same day, the regiment left Rolla to begin another campaign to Springfield. Led by Samuel R. Curtis and designated the Army of the Southwest, the Federals again occupied Springfield without a significant battle. Unlike before, the advance continued. Kircher and the 12th Missourians were keyed up for their first action, "ready to fight like lions," but the Rebels gave them no opportunity to bloody themselves.[33] After pushing into Arkansas, Curtis encamped his army near the state line at Sugar Creek.

---

[29] Diary, Oct. 25, 26, 1861.
[30] Diary, Nov. 10, 1861.
[31] Diary, Dec. 20, 1861; Jan. 1, 2, 1862.
[32] Muster rolls, Otto Schadt, Hugo Wangelin, Jacob Kaercher, Albert Affleck, and Henry Kircher service records, NA.
[33] Diary, Feb. 16, 1862.

Sigel marched his two divisions farther south, three and one-half miles from Bentonville, to a place called McKissick's Farm.

Soon after, Kircher saw his first battle; it proved to be a spectacular conflict for the 12th Missouri. The Rebel army turned on Curtis with unexpected speed, nearly catching Sigel before he could rejoin the Southwestern army at Sugar Creek. Sigel held Kircher's regiment and other troops at Bentonville to serve as a rearguard for his retrograde move north. Confederate cavalry sparred with this small force when it fell back from Bentonville. The "galant 250 Lions of the 12th Mo." performed steadily in their introduction to combat, keeping the enemy at bay while Sigel deftly handled a battery to tip the balance in his favor. Kircher and his regiment were saved to take an even more conspicuous part in the fighting to come.[34]

The Battle of Pea Ridge culminated the following day, March 7, although it was touch and go for Kircher. The Rebels outflanked Curtis's position at Sugar Creek and attacked on two fronts; Osterhaus and Jefferson C. Davis blocked them on the left, near Leetown, by holding firm with artillery and infantry. Kircher's regiment, on the right of Osterhaus's line, was one of the first units to respond to a near Rebel breakthrough between Osterhaus's and Davis's divisions.

It was an important crisis, one that could have fractured Federal resistance at Leetown and endangered Curtis's entire army. Osterhaus wheeled his old regiment around to meet the danger; at the same time, Kircher also responded. Affleck had been hit in the leg earlier that day and Company A was under the direction of its acting second lieutenant.[35] Kircher behaved like a veteran. Facetiously, he later claimed credit for the maneuver. "I will say it. *I* did it and saved the day. . . . I made a move, a simple one but the right one, and commanded 'by the right flank by file left,' and carrying it out myself, split back again, first caught sight of Osterhaus and Wangelin far on the left flank of the regiment when they were pointing at the secesh that took our cannons. But I had already given the command and I fired two shots myself while running in order to indicate to the others what they should do. . . . It went double quick in the new direction, and the secesh were strangled by our bullets. . . . The day was ours."[36]

After helping to save the army on March 7, Kircher and his men formed with the rest of Curtis's army on March 8 to drive away the remaining Rebels. The fighting proved to be a smashing confirmation of the previous day's success. Kircher's Company A advanced as skirmishers, along

---

[34] Diary, Mar. 6, 1862.

[35] Casualty sheet, undated, Albert Affleck service record, NA.

[36] The quotation is from an undated fragment attached to Kircher's Nov. 28, 1862 letter to his mother. The Federal guns he mentioned belonged to Battery A, 2d Illinois Light Artillery. They were recaptured. *The War of the Rebellion: A Compilation of the Official Records of the Union and Confederate Armies* ser. 1, vol. 8 (Washington, D.C., 1883), 246; hereafter cited as *OR*. All volumes cited are in series 1.

with other units, and "opened an outragious fire" that scattered its opponents. The 12th Missouri picked up three cannons and a silk Rebel flag as trophies, and established for itself a reputation as a unit of hard-fighting Germans.[37] Pea Ridge marked the end of serious Confederate attempts to control Missouri and Kircher played a satisfying part in it.

Spectacular as it was, Pea Ridge did not lead to further glory for Curtis's small army. Arkansas was stripped of most Confederate troops soon afterward to bolster defenses east of the Mississippi, leaving Kircher with few organized foes. He was assigned to Company C as second lieutenant on March 19.[38] Soon afterward, the Army of the Southwest began a long spring and summer of dismal floundering through the wilds of central Arkansas that sorely tried its morale. A rugged, semideveloped area, the state produced little more than footsores, malarial disease, and ruthless bushwhackers.

The army reached Batesville by May 3. While most of it rested there, Osterhaus's division trudged farther south, trying to open a line of march to Little Rock. Kircher came no closer to the state capital of Arkansas than Searcy Landing on the Little Red River. There, forty-nine miles away, he and the rest of Osterhaus's command worked as hard at finding enough food in the "swampy and mirey Bottomland" as they did fighting the numerous Rebel guerrillas.[39] It was a frustrating time, so near a symbolic goal but held back by a cautious army commander unwilling to risk a further advance until he became certain of his overstretched supply lines.

The stalemate lasted for a month before Osterhaus finally took his men back to Batesville. There, Kircher wrote the second of his extant letters from the 12th Missouri. It testified to the disenchantment with army life, intensified in Kircher's case by Curtis's unsatisfactory campaigning, that nearly every soldier felt at some time.

Camp near Batesville June 14 62

Dear Mother!

It is most heartily boring to lie in camp and hear nothing but the everlasting griping. All are dissatisfied from the soldier up to the general; and then there has been the beginning of a quite significant heat. And there is the demand of Uncle Sam to pay up the clothing accounts (which are still due to U.S., after which nothing is left to most soldiers of their 2 months wages).[40] The strongest af-

---

[37] Diary, Mar. 8, 1862.

[38] Muster rolls, Henry Kircher service record, NA.

[39] Diary, May 22, 1862.

[40] According to army regulations, the cost of extra suits of clothes was deducted from the men's pay. The 12th and 17th Missouri, however, refused to sign the payroll, a protest against "that chronic complaint, rotten, worthless clothing, by which many claim to have been swindled." *St. Louis Daily Missouri Democrat,* June 20, 1862.

fect in the complaint department is the great supply of whiskey, which the various sutlers were so good to supply. When one puts all this together and looks at it, one develops such an antipathy and abhorrence that one would, with the greatest pleasure, turn his back on the whole soldiering business and crawl into his tent. To leave, go home, which I would rather do, I cannot under the present circumstances.

There are in the whole regiment, as is generally said, 3 cliques: namely, the Belleville or Illinois clique and the St. Louis or Missouri, which they call the misery clique, and then the neutral. That is the bastard, because they consist of the undecided and drifters. The main spring of all this is envy. No one can see another advance or get along well. And all kinds of means are set in motion, even of the lowest, meanest sort, to bring him down who undertakes to feel satisfied.

Oh! now, yes, now I truly feel it and am infinitely grateful for the good upbringing which you gave me and the excellent example with which you always went before your children through good and evil fortune, in joy and discomfort. It is wrong of me that I make this comment only now, since I have always felt this. But that is how it is, that one only then recognizes the good which was given to one and one always enjoys after one has left to know more of the world and its wretched creatures.

But it is not yet too late to make up the neglected confession. We children have and, God willing, will have the irreplaceable fortune to enjoy our parents further, constantly making the effort with fresh and untiring zeal to lead us forward in the right path.

But I see I always only encourage and can myself, at present, only serve with words. But if your son Henry has it in his power, he will be with you before many months have passed, to work together with a new spirit with his siblings to make us all worthy of you.

Your loyal son Henry

Kircher remained at Batesville until the end of June, when the Army of the Southwest took the only feasible direction left. The southward advance had proved impractical, a northward withdrawal was unthinkable, so Curtis led his men east and south along the curving White River to contact Union supply boats. Rebel guerrillas blocked the roads with trees, but Kircher's most serious enemy proved to be the Arkansas summer. As he struggled across the streams and swampy ground, the "exceedingly hot" sun ruined his

Independence Day, "mainly celibrated by us with swetting and coursing on account of the scarcity of water, and plenty of dust."[41]

As if the elements were not enough to trouble the poor soldiers, Federal authorities found it impossible to coordinate logistics. When Curtis reached Clarendon on July 9, he discovered no boats and little prospect of meeting any. Unwilling to wait, the army set out cross-county for Helena on the Mississippi and the sure opportunity of contacting supply ships with food and other articles. It was a short march of a few days but probably the hardest of the entire campaign. Most of Curtis's soldiers felt, as did Kircher, a great sense of relief when the wide, muddy waters of the Mississippi came into view with loaded boats waiting for hungry men. "We were certaine that the world still stood as it formerly did, although the Confedred States had taken with Consumtion. Kill 'm quick."[42]

Nearly a year had passed since Kircher had crossed the Mississippi to St. Louis and signed his name on the rolls of Osterhaus's regiment. During that time, he had taken part in three campaigns, fought in a stirring three-day battle and logged 1,231 miles of arduous marching.[43] The young recruit was still young, but had become something more: a toughened and experienced soldier.

---

[41] Diary, July 4, 1862.
[42] Diary, July 14, 1862.
[43] The computation of miles marched is in the flap of Kircher's last Civil War diary.

CHAPTER TWO

"As Gay and Happy as Possible"

The temporary shelter Curtis hoped to find at Helena became a lengthy rest as July turned into August and the summer gave way to fall. Like most of his comrades, Kircher found little to do, so he occupied his time with writing letters. The extant documents form the advance of a long correspondence that extended over the next fifteen months.

Camp near Helena, August 2, 62

Dear Father!

In order to bring our correspondence back on the track, which was almost beginning to get very lame and threatened almost to become past tense, I am writing once again.

Since our last exchange of letters quite a few changes have taken place in our glorious Fatherland as well as in myself; with the difference that I was luckier than the first and you probably know better what went on in it than I do, for you have more opportunity to hear about everything. But still, I have heard and experienced enough to make the gall rise up to my teeth from the selfishness, weakness, short-sightedness, cowardice, ignorance, indeed dumb dumbness of most of our chief leaders of the good and untiring soldiers. But I place trust in some few generals and it won't take long until we again hear encouraging news from these few.

If Siegel has a chance to show his present soldiers that an "r" instead of an "l" belongs at the end of his name he can terrify the enemy, make them flee and, as befits traitors, capture them just by going out into the battlefield.[1] His shooting wagons don't even need to thunder. His soldiers will follow him even if he goes with one against a dozen. At least we did it and would do it again if we had the good fortune of being led by him. It never occurred to any of us to be afraid for himself because of this or that. He did not teach us to know fear, only to obey him, obey him blindly and to

---

[1] "Sieger" means "victor" in German. Sigel had been promoted to major general after Pea Ridge and had been given command of a corps in Virginia. He omitted the first "e" from his name but Kircher insisted on using it.

win. Long live Siegel! And woe to him who hesitates to follow him or who places any obstacle in his modest, laboriously earned path to glory and the eternal memory of his Fatherland and the honor of its citizens!

Now to another head not so much crowned with laurels, namely that of your Henry.

It stands as ever, solidly and unshakebly on the powerful machine builder's shoulders. And with the help of his strong right one, he seems to work his way through all obstacles in the end in order to prove to his own by and by that he is worthy and proud of them.

In short, my long awaited commission for 2nd lieutenant finally arrived, dated the 19th of March, so from then on to get $105 monthly: quite pleasant! In addition, the satisfaction that I am really an officer and no longer half of one.

I hardly had my patent when Col. Wangelin came to me and asked if I would take the position of adjutant, as J[oseph] Ledergerber was acting adjutant and had petitioned to be relieved of it. I hesitated a little and then he said I was the only one he considered capable of filling the position. With Affleck's persuasion, I agreed then and became on July 17th acting adjutant of the 12th regt. Missouri Infantry Volunteers. Everything went quite well and fine.

Now suddenly, as I had feared, General Osterhaus comes here again (last night) and brings a commission for J. Ledergerber as adjutant of the regiment and I must now go back to my company of course.[2]

Now it was a prank that Osterhaus played on me without knowing it, for he didn't know that I was acting adjutant. And kindly Col. W., as he does everything else, was daydreaming, asleep, or he wanted to play a practical joke on me; but I believe he is too dumb for the latter and I therefore pardon him for his trick. But at least I am 2nd lieutenant in Company C and perhaps I will climb even farther. In the meantime, you will have to be satisfied with the one.

I can still only draw money as a sergeant, since I am listed as such on the muster roll. The next time we are paid out I can draw it all though. Therefore, I am touching my friends for a little in the meantime.

I would like to visit you sometime, but it seems that it won't

---

[2] Osterhaus had returned to the army from a sick leave.

work yet because everybody must be sick or must know how to pretend to be before getting a leave. Therefore you will have to wait until I have learned how to deceive or there is an opportunity to get another kind of leave. The former will probably take a long time or not occur at all. Therefore patience, it will happen somehow.

Greet everybody, everybody many thousand times from your obedient son Henry

Camp Helena Arks. September 2nd 1862[3]

Dear Brother!

Your kind epistol of the 26th last month, in companion with on[e] of Joe same date, I just had the pleasure of running over with my eyes, and find that you are getting along as gay as ever, and commit as many outrages as before and am happy to see that in mostly all your enjoyments you generally have more luck than sence. For instance, how easily might those Coaldiggers not have appreciated your joke, when you young chaps intruded into their wedding enjoyments, and treated you according to their impressions quite right, in giving you some black eyes and several tips with the point of their boots [.] Ai George Ai how would you have like that, but luckeyly it turned out diferent for you.

But what is the reason you do anything of the kind if you want to keep it secret; you ought never do anything, George, what would embaras you, to let your parents know [;] no, George never, never do anything that you were not ready to relate at any time to your, or better our parents, with all its particulars! It is not right, and you are now by de by old enough to make a distinction between right and wrong, and follow the path of the former, and let the path of the latter with all its windings and temptations go by with dispise.

The time passes devilish slow with us here, doing hardly anything al daylong but read or play chess or make some foolishness together or perhaps talk of the old times and our school trick & etc. such a thing will all do for a little while but for 3 years it is rather tedious. It is singular, although one day or each day passes so slow with us, but a week or a month seems allways to be over in less than no time.

I wished I new how I could manage to get some boocks about

---

[3] This is Kircher's only extant letter to his brother George. It was written in English.

Machinery, Algebra Geometry and Physiologi for I have now for instance plenty of time to study which would do me some good [.] I ame afraid after those three years are over I will have forgotten every thing in my line (machinery) [.] In fact I have some idea to save money enough, so I might go to study in some institution, which strikes my line. I suppose I ought to be able to save about 1000 dollars in two years [;] Uncle Sam is liberal, he pays me about 105 dollars a month [.] of course everything that an officer is obliged to buy or have, is hell and damnation heigh [.] the darn sutlers must all be rich by this time, or else spent their money as fast as they make it.

With all those necessary expences and perhaps a few for luxury I still hope to save about half or near half of my sallery.

I am glad to hear that Willy is learning piano now, for I have often already felt how pleasant it is to know some instrument [;] it will do to pass time when sole or in company, and make you always so much more wellcome in a gay circle than otherwise.[4] Were I in your place I would strive to learn it still, be it piano or even singing and gittare would be less expensive and quicker understood [.] think over it and you will find I am right and you but to lazy to learn?

Oh' I know you by heart old stick [;] but if you can get over it you will be thankfull to me after you ar older I am sure.

My best respects to all whom it may concern. your brother,

and true friend Henry Kircher

Camp Helena Arks. September 3d 1862

Dear Mother!

Yesterday evening Bert suddenly gave me a letter from you dated the 22nd of May, when we were still in Batesville that is. Well, he brought me a lot of joy anyway, for something from you is always welcome with all my heart, whether it comes early or late.

I don't know myself what the names of the different books are, but I would like to have one on Mechanics, Geometry, Physics and Algebra. I think it best if the books are in the English language, as the terms of the various things, etc., are different from the German and are more usable here in the first than in the latter language. Then you could also send me the *Book of Nature* by Schröder, I believe. It must be at home among the books. I had it

---

4 Will F. Kircher was Henry's much younger brother.

for Rau when I went to school there.⁵ It is an instructive book about all of natural science, Geology, Physiology, Astronomy, etc., although not exhaustively; still, sufficient to refresh everything that I formerly knew and perhaps increase it some.

You can send them at any opportunity, perhaps with Oster-haus as soon as he has finished mildewing away in St. Louis.⁶ Somebody is always going and people like us could kick the bucket on the spot before getting a leave. Eh bien, le temps approcherat où je suis mon maitre, où je puit avoir moi tete, où il ne faut pas que je dance, comme on pfeift. [Oh well, the time is coming when I am my own master, when I can have my own way, when I don't have to dance to somebody else's tune.]

Greet everybody a thousand times from

your son Henry Kircher

Camp Helena Ark. September 8th 1862

Dear, good Mother!

Your last letter confirmed the uneasiness that I have felt for a few days; but instead of calming me down, of course it increased my uneasiness. Poor George must certainly have to endure a lot, and you no less. May God grant that he and you all pass his test.

But write, anybody, even a few lines, just the changes in his illness. For being so in doubt about the danger that a beloved member of the family is suspended in is unbearable. I don't know; I never have any rest, never stay anyplace very long, go from one tent to another and don't find what I am looking for in any. Oh, please write.

Yesterday I was in a little better mood, wondering if George was doing better too. But today I am again burning just as much from desire and uncertainty to get news as before.

Oh, if I had been able to forsee this I would have tried to come on recruiting service instead of rejecting it.⁷ Then I would be with you on Engelmann Street. But who can predict all this?

I don't know anything at all to write, except that the desire to

---

⁵ Carl Rau operated a private school in Belleville in the early 1850s. He later achieved an international reputation as an archeologist and anthropologist, and became curator of the Smithsonian's Department of Archeology in 1881. *Belleville Advocate,* Dec. 2, 1898. Walter Hough, "Charles Rau," *Dictionary of American Biography* 15:388–89.
⁶ Osterhaus had taken another sick leave.
⁷ The regiment detailed several officers and men on recruiting service to St. Louis and other points in late August, 1862. Hess, "The 12th Missouri Infantry," 74.

hear something from you hits me so much. I think it comes on more whenever I write again.

Write, write, write! Even if it is the worst.

A thousand greetings and my innermost wishes for recovery! May God grant Uncle Adolph good luck and skill in restoring George.

Your sad Henry

At the time Kircher wrote his admonitory letter of September 2 to George, his brother lay mortally ill. He died on September 3 of "brain fever," at age 17.[8] Kircher's mother faced the difficult task of writing Henry about the tragedy.

Belleville September 8, 1862

My Henry!

George is now gently resting. We mourn him deeply, deeply. Not to receive still more gay letters from you to him you can hardly believe.

I feel for you doubly all the pains and all suffering that you have to bear all by yourself. We are together, we could nurse him together in the five horrible days of his illness. And you have to suffer the bitterness of the pain all by yourself. But you are good and strong and you will not give yourself over to too great an amount of pain. See, I don't do it either. I keep myself erect and I already try not to fight against my fate on account of your father, who is striving for the same philosophy but who is indescribably bent and who looks very miserable. We indeed have to help each other. Uncle is also taking it very hard; and Loulou, you know her feelings. George's death has made a very serious impression on Joe; if it will remain, we will see.

As I have heard, Albert Affleck is supposed to have a daguerreotype of George. Since we are not in the possession of a picture, he will certainly be happy to make an old mother happy. I will never forget it if he is so dear and gives it to me.

For you, my dear heart, I can do at the present nothing but write to you even more diligently than usual.

For us all, I have done what I feel is the greatest consolation, to write to Gen. Osterhaus and ask for a furlough for you; where-

---

[8] *Belleville Advocate,* Sept. 5, 1862. When Goedeking informed August Mersy of George's illness, the latter wrote, "After your description, I believe he died from *sunstroke.*" Mersy to Goedeking, Sept. 10, 1862.

upon he and his wife have answered very dear and full of sympathy. And he addressed G[eneral] Steele on account of that. I hope he will succeed in giving you back to us for a short time; father especially needs you badly.[9]

About myself, I don't care to talk much. Father is my main concern. He is indeed lonesome and his hearing is very bad. And under these conditions your brother's death was a horrible blow for him. Father had hoped to be more free of the burden of his business in a few years, and he hoped to see George as his very energetic replacement in the store.

Willy said that he wanted to go into the store after he had learned enough and father really takes him along already. He has a very dear and understanding nature. George's death has awakened the best resolutions in him; he wants to follow and not to fight with Hetty so much more.[10]

All acquaintances compete with each other to show us their friendship. I have really not known that so many people are interested in us. George was very popular even with older people, and of course especially with the young ones; they mourn him openly and with all their heart.

Bill Wangelin, who was one of the pallbearers, had to sink him down into the earth with many tears.[11] And the soil will seem light to George, because only hands of his friends closed up the grave. Mr. Noettling, on your father's wish, spoke a few words on the grave and the dead silence proved the impact. Amen.

The situation of the country is nothing to be happy about. Treason in all corners, corruption up to the smallest employees of the machine of the state. Waste and spoiling by negligence; they are doing this to our patriotic and brave army. So this is how it looks at home!

The heart bleeds wherever you look. If the people of the North, driven by a feeling of noble revenge, don't rise up and help themselves and step on the head of the snake of treason, then I say we will be lost and the tyrants hold the flag high over the murdered freedom!

---

[9] Osterhaus could do little about Kircher's leave while he was off duty, sick in St. Louis. Frederick Steele commanded the army at Helena at that time.

[10] Hetty was Kircher's much younger sister.

[11] William Wangelin, a nephew of the regimental commander, was a corporal in the 12th Missouri serving on detached duty as one of Osterhaus's orderlies. Muster rolls, William Wangelin service record, NA.

From Col. M[ersy] we also received a few days ago a letter, wherein he asked about Ge[orge] and says that he has the position of a lieutenant ready and waiting for him.[12]

At the fairground are lying 3 companies of Col. Niles, his regiment, who is organizing one and whose rendezvous is Belleville.[13] They seem to be harmless young boys, mostly young Americans.

Now, goodbye my dear son. Do all you can for your health and for your parents as faithfully as you have always done it. All greet you heartily.

With a heartfelt kiss from
your faithful mother.

Augusta's stoic sentences might have been soothing to the young lieutenant, but before he received them the bitterness of loss made his life away from loved ones miserable.

Camp Helena Sept. 9th 1862

Dear Parents, Uncle, Brothers and Sisters!

Col. Wangelin just gave me the sad news that our dear George has been torn from our midst. Oh! if I could just be in your midst to mix my tears with yours, such sorrow is easier to bear together than when scattered in this way. Why didn't I go recruiting? I would have seen George once more; indeed, I would have seen his suffering, the struggle with death that not all of us have to fight. But why is it not that all those who love one another, also everybody suffering together from this enemy, can't be victorious? Torn away right in his finest, happiest years of life; it might be well and good, for he never had any trouble and sorrows and his soul is probably carrying on in eternity the pleasures that he began on earth on an even greater scale. But we can only mourn the loss from our midst and console ourselves with hope.

And we, my good brothers and sisters, have a double obligation. First, the pain from the loss of our dear brother that we feel just as much as our parents. Second, we must support our parents and Uncle, who was always a father to us, with all of our powers. For we are younger and more resilient and can therefore stand more, for our spirit is more strongly supported by our body. Let

[12] After its reorganization, Mersy's 9th Illinois participated in the battles of Fort Donelson and Shiloh and the advance to Corinth. In the late summer of 1862, it performed garrison duty in southwestern Tennessee and northern Mississippi. Frederick H. Dyer, *A Compendium of the War of the Rebellion,* vol. 3 (1908; reprint, New York, 1959), 1047.

[13] Colonel Nathan Niles organized the 130th Illinois Infantry.

your tears flow as I let mine flow; it is balm for the same and re-lieves us. But take care of your parents and Uncle with doubled at-tention. I can only help with words, if it is a help. However, you have the good fortune of being together and can be effective in that way. Namely, I tremble when I think of our dear mother, whose health has been bad in the last few years. You must support her in every-thing and in all things that can bring her relief, pleasure or diver-sion. I can't say any more, for it is hard to console when you are disconsolate yourself.

In sorrow and in joy, your Henry

Camp near Helena Ark. September 12th 1862

Dear Mother!

Everything and everything else that I tried was in vain, and I won't be able to visit you all yet. It would have to be so.

According to the last order from Washington, only one soldier can go on leave, if his life directly depends on it; that is, just on ac-count of sickness, and I'm not sick.

However, Osterhaus can do a lot in this respect; indeed, I would say he can let me go if he wants to.

There are methods of cicumventing the order if a general wants to. He can send somebody on official business to take care of something. It's quite natural that it is harder for an officer to get a leave, as there are fewer of them and they are missed more and are recognized immediately everywhere, assuming they go dressed as required by law.

Col. Wangelin has been laboring just as long as we have been here on leave and can't get away.

Now I don't know where to begin if some opportunity pres-ents itself. I wouldn't waste any second though and seize it with haste, for I desire nothing more than to see you all again. Would to God the war were over! Then I could come home again to bear whatever might befall us with you all. Such a sorrow hits a person doubly hard. However, if one can mix his tears with those of another, that relieves the heart. But if one is sitting isolated in a tent, no matter how funny this all sounds, then they burn the cheeks instead of cooling them, and such tears taste bitter, very bitter.

But sometime, indeed perhaps soon, it will be permitted for me to come to you all again. The war can't last forever! Oh me, now it is almost all the same to me who is victorious or who is defeated, if I were only free.

A thousand and again a thousand greetings to you all, all.

Your sad Henry

II.

September 13th 1862

I kept the first sheet until today, as I considered it too short a letter for our correspondence. But strangely, I can't find any words or material to write now, whereas earlier I could have sat for days and chatted with you without giving the pen even 5 minutes rest. Nothing interests me anymore except your letters, which, yes, which never would be able to come often enough even if they came steadily from morning to evening, from evening to morning.

If I didn't still have you, everything would be all the same to me in this deserted world. How little did I think of George's illness, much less of his————, when I sent the last letter to him. When I think how happy I still was then, I cringe. While he was struggling with death, I sat happily with Joe and Bert, chatting, not suspecting anything bad. So it goes in the world; some shed tears of joy, others tears of sorrow.

But this all comes from a higher power than is given to mankind to exercise in this world or to thwart. Therefore we must quietly bear what God the Father requires of us.

If I knew for sure that I possibly wouldn't have to go back to the field, I would do my best to get away. Then I would be able to support you in everything with my powers. I would go into the store if it pleased father better, or to a turning lathe or whatever his wishes are. They are also my wishes. But I would be in danger of following the soldier's life once again. I think it is better this way than to start all anew, don't you think?

Bert tells me he doesn't have a picture of George. They wanted to get pictures taken of each other but George didn't have any time to do it, and so it got forgotten. If he had had one, I would have seen it a long time ago.

If I could only paint, you would soon have a finished picture of George. How vividly I can see his friendly features before my eyes, more accurate than a picture can be.

A thousand and another thousand sincere greetings to all.

Henry

In the midst of Kircher's distress, Colonel Wangelin kindly extended a helping hand. There were, indeed, ways to circumvent the restriction on leaves of absence. On September 14, Kircher received Wangelin's order to proceed to St. Louis in order to forward all regimental property to Helena. He left aboard the steamer *Empress* the next day and reached Belleville on September 18. Kircher did not record whether he performed the task that served as his mission north, but he did take the opportunity to spend four welcome weeks with his family.[14]

By the time he was ready to return, his division had left the ennui of Helena. Loaded aboard steamboats, it rode upriver to Ste. Genevieve, Missouri, sixty miles south of St. Louis. From there the men marched to Ironton to block a fictitious Rebel advance into eastern Missouri. Strategically unnecessary, the shift of a substantial portion of Steele's force nevertheless allowed the men to escape Arkansas.

Kircher learned of the move and decided to head straight for Ironton. He arrived on October 17 and stayed in the Pilot Knob Hotel until the division caught up with him two days later. The painful loss of his brother was expiated by the visit to Belleville, and he felt "at home again" when he caught sight of the 12th Missouri.[15]

The following month was, for soldiers, an idyllic rest secure from the guerrillas, heat, and disease of Arkansas. Kircher had been promoted to first lieutenant of Company K on September 5, a fact the immediacy of George's death prevented him from relating in his correspondence.[16] The advancement made little difference in his work load; he had little more to do at Ironton than sample the peach brandy made by area farmers, play chess with Sgt. Charles Hilgard of Company A, and practice revolver shooting. Casimir Andel, German-born Belleviller and second lieutenant of Company A, joined his target exercies. On one such outing east of Pilot Knob, they found a tortoise and scratched their names on its shell. The proximity to St. Louis encouraged a two-way traffic; regimenters scampered off on leave while hometown friends traveled south to visit. Financial considerations pulled most soldiers back to Ironton. "They begin to smell mice? Who is absent at Muster don't receive any Pay."[17]

As during the idle period at Batesville the preceding June, feuding between the Missourians and Illinoisans in the unit came to the fore at Ironton. The new regimental colors, provided by the loyal women of Belleville, became the focal point of interstate jealousy.

Camp Ironton Nov. 10th 1862

Dear Mother!

Now it is once again the anniversary of our presence. My only

---

[14] Diary, Sept. 14, 15, 18, 1862.
[15] Diary, Oct. 17, 19, 1862.
[16] Muster rolls, Henry Kircher service record, NA.
[17] Diary, Oct. 21, 26, 28, 29, 1862.

wish is that we celebrate it properly many more times, but no more times without you.[18]

In this world everything may be set up quite well, but there is still a *but*; it could be better and nicer. Above all there should be many more good, good, honest people than bad. But unfortunately, the latter sort of individual is by far stronger and more numerously represented than the first-mentioned.

But what good does this all do now? I won't get it changed. I am satisfied with you and with me and with those who don't bother me, no matter what they do or don't do, so long as they don't tread too near. Or else he can withdraw in heat and flight. I don't know. I'm so angry that I almost can't write anything. The reason:

Yesterday, there was a big review here before Genr [John W.] Davidson. Bert, Joe L[edergerber], Casimir and I wanted the Col. to name somebody flagbearer and to hand over the flag so that we could also appear with a flag. But fat *Niks* [Colonel Wangelin] said that the General [Osterhaus] had promised it to this one and that one. Whoever has nothing to give has nothing to promise. If the flag weren't in Joe's hands Bert and I would have gotten it handed over [to be used in the review]. But L[ieutenant] Hormann again [intervened], since [that] wouldn't have been according to their wishes. The whole story is that no Belleviller should carry it, and the wish of Hormann was exactly this.[19]

It would perhaps be effective if Joe and about a half a hundred more sent a suitable correction to our supreme commander. "Some how" it has to be done, and until Osterhaus arrives we will make hell hot enough for the fat one. And if that all doesn't help, we'll take [the flag] away secretly and send it back to you. Then the fat one, Osterhaus, and all those who have nothing to say but still remain in the dirt can run after it. Then they can see where they can get one.

In general, the St. Louisans are in a very poisonous mood against the Bellevillers; but it is only envy and now too late. We have them pretty much in our power. We came into the regiment with 6 officers. Now we have 13 or 14 nothing but young, vigorous "don't care a damn Belleville boys, who won't be run over by any

---

[18] Kircher shared his mother's birthday.

[19] Kircher carefully hedged his written commentary on this feud. His reference to the key person, as near as can be deciphered, is to Theodore Hormann, a Missourian who served as 2d lieutenant of Company E.

man" men. This is what is bugging the gentlemen; we are getting, no, we are already too powerful for them.

Bert said that I would be the first one who became 21 without getting drunk. When I came into his tent in the evening, there stood a box of wine waiting impatiently for Joe, Bert, and Casimir. We spent a pleasant evening, and despite the wine I became 21 without getting drunk. I don't even know what it is [to be drunk].

A thousand hearty greetings to all.

Your true son Henry

The division left Ironton on November 12, reversing its march of the previous month and heading for Ste. Genevieve. Higher authorities had had ample time to regret the division's transfer north, and they decided to return it to Helena. The men pitched camp at Ste. Genevieve on November 14 and the next day the 12th Missouri formally received its new colors during a brigade drill. Joseph Ledergerber also read an address to the regiment sent by the same Belleville ladies who supplied the flag, adding a few words "which [were] very proper for the occasion." A lunch and wine party followed, attended by most officers of the division. In one regard, the Missourians beat the Illinoisans; they managed to have one of their own appointed to carry the flag. As Kircher ruefully put it, "the wish of the Ladies . . . entirely disrespected."[20]

The 12th Missouri boarded the steamer *John Warner* on November 16 but not before Kircher had acquired what many Federal officers felt indispensable, a black servant. He engaged Louis to perform cooking and maid duties, and the ex-slave remained with him until the end of his field service. On November 17, the *Warner* pointed downriver and sped south.[21]

Camp in State Mississippi via Helena
November 24th 1862

Dear Mother!

Just to prove to you that I and we are all alive and well, we arrived the day before yesterday in Helena and yesterday [went to] the Mississippi side, where we then grabbed our things out of the steamboat and pitched our camp. The whole journey, although boring, got underway very well; only we got stuck on a sandbar one day 50 miles above Memphis but gradually worked our way loose.

We were surprised (Genr. [Alvin P.] Hovey too, who didn't know of our coming) that we went into camp here again, for we were all looking foward to storming Vicksburg, which it now ap-

---

[20] Diary, Nov. 12, 14, 15, 1862.
[21] Diary, Nov. 16, 17, 1862.

pears that nobody intends to attack. There are a large number of troops here, certainly 40 or 50,000, and they keep coming and there are still more expected. Now this can't be all there is to it. It is probably a deep, anxious lull before a storm, a mighty eruption that will flood the South not with lava, but significantly with Dutchmen and Yankees. If the winter is used well by the North and the proper blows are dealt out, we will have a fine spring.

There are a lot of parrots here in Mississippi. People buy them. They are so pretty: red heads, yellow-gold collars around their necks and then into green for the rest of their bodies, sometimes lighter, sometimes darker, really very beautiful. I am enclosing a little wing feather for you. They are about as big as a wild dove.

A thousand hearty greetings to all and to everyone who can look me in the eyes without blinking.

Your true son Henry

Camp Steele vis-à-vis Helena Arkansas
November 28th 1862

Chere Mama!

Although I still don't have an answer to my last letter I will write you anyway, as there are surely letters from you underway and you like to see my handwriting so well. Besides, I want to tell you various things.

First, there was great consternation and cogitation about how we can circumvent or at least alleviate a certain order from Washington. Namely, no regiment shall have more than 6 wagons (formerly 24), each 2 soldiers 1 shelter tent, just one piece of sailcloth spread out, and each officer 1 such tent. Soldiers shall carry theirs buckled in their pack with a blanket, and no officer shall carry more than a *reasonable* (how many is that? what does that mean?) number of blankets, together with a small valise or carpetbag as baggage. Of the 6 wagons, one is exclusively for the hospital, a second for the regimental staff (colonel, lieutenant colonel, major and adjutant), the other four for the regiment; that is for provisions and officers' baggage (which would be best to be limited to a mere nothing or, if possible, a little less).[22]

Now if this order should really be carried out as strictly as it

---

[22] William T. Sherman incorporated those guidelines in his General Order No. 6, dated Dec. 13, 1862, when he prepared the troops at Memphis and Helena for campaigning. *OR*, vol. 17, pt. 1, 617–18.

says, there is nothing left for me and all the rest but to send our whole rummage home or to leave it standing and to leave its fate in those hands. But I have none of the latter in mind, for as soon as I know how or when I will send my chest & etc. to Bremermann.[23] If it gets lost underway, well, it probably will be just as good or as bad as would have happened here. But it has already traversed the way alone once and will be able to do it again.

If this order would contribute to fighting the war more energetically or if it would help end it more quickly, then I would not waste a word about it and if it had to be would bear my pack & etc. as well as any soldier should. The reason is given that it is to make the trains shorter. Will the train be shorter if we take away X number of wagons at one end and add them on again at the other? Stupidity, for however many wagons less we have the commissary and subsistance as well as the division quartermaster train must have that many more. For instead of 10–15 days' rations, now we can carry 4–5 at the most with our 4 regimental wagons and the commissary train has to carry the rest. We've got to have it, for there is no existence without food, and the secesh look too dry and tough for me to believe that they would give up a nice beefsteak.

By the way, Uncle Sam is quite right; he should only keep us a short while [longer] and the secesh will have to suffer all the more, not us. Oh no, we ain't green nor small taters, especially the 12th. They have kept distinguishing themselves, but not yet with stupidity or an empty stomach; and we won't do it, furthermore. All that is certain is that the dear Lord must be awfully merciful to the secesh, or else it will be too bad for them when they fall into our hands.

Now something that may surprise you. Last evening Bert, Joe and I were sitting together and talking about all kinds of remarkable countries, cities & etc., when we suddenly got the idea that if we could see all this sometime it would be much better than just hearing about it. And we decided unanimously that from now until the end of the war we would set aside as much money as possible. As soon as we were mustered out and then were sufficiently prepared, to travel to Europe and journey to every place that was worth seeing for as long as our money that we had saved up would last. Wouldn't that be nice, to sail around the world as a young clover until the wind blows all the sails away and we then will calmly and

---

[23] Bremermann was a St. Louis merchant patronized by the Germans of St. Clair County.

complacently burden our necks again with the bourgeois yoke as satisfied and well-traveled young people?

You surely have nothing against it, for when you're young you've got to go out in the world; but if you're old you stay home of your own accord. The war will probably last long enough yet that we will each have saved approximately $1,000, and then we can make a little excursion. Even if it's only halfway across the sea and back, we've got to travel. Josie ought to go to Mersy as an aide-de-camp, and then she can also set aside enough to come along. We would rather take Loulou, though of course without requiring any extra contribution. Who knows? If Uncle hears about it, he might even get the urge to travel again at his age.

We three will not spare anything venturesome, for afterward the dogs of war can break loose with a rush.

About General Davidson (son of David, therefore one of our people). He may be in his thirties, dark hair, a long straight mustache with a twist on the end with a little gray here and there, a long face with a rather outstanding chin. A high, broad forehead, prominent smelling tool and small, dark, rather piercing eyes.

Was formerly Captain in 2d Regiment U.S. Dragoons, regulars. Looks quite intelligent, determined and firm. In all, he impressed me pretty much and I believe he may well be a very good soldier, but can't say much about him. I haven't seen him since he reviewed us in Pilot Knob. As far as I know, he commanded the troops that went by land from there to Helena, the former [Frederick] Steele's division, as well as the cavalry that belongs to our division. They haven't arrived here yet.[24]

Many greetings to everybody and everybody.

Your true Henry

Camp Steele, Mississippi December 3rd 1862

Dear Mother!

"There is a screw loose somewheres." You write that I haven't written extensively enough [about] what you sent with Capt. [Fred Tell] Ledergerber. So, a letter with a photograph, the razor knife and strop, "expressly manufactured for Gilchrist's razors," 2 pieces of coconut oil soap, a shaving brush, a cup of shaving soap with a

---

[24] Davidson had been a captain in the prewar 1st U.S. Cavalry and became major of the 2d U.S. Cavalry in November, 1861. Francis B. Heitman, *Historical Register and Dictionary of the United States Army,* vol. 1 (1903; reprint, Urbana, 1965), 355. His infantry and cavalry marched to southern Missouri and never rejoined the Osterhaus division, then led by Steele.

mirror on the lid and the box itself with two tickets and a couple leaves of various plants, and then two bars of chocolate manufactured by Berchelmann and Kempff.

As far as I can remember, this was all wrapped in a newspaper and well tied with string and wrapped in a second piece of paper, but this time good wrapping paper and then tied again with strong gray hemp cord whose both ends were united on a button.

There is nothing new here concerning God and the world. At the most in the night a few shots from the pickets, sometimes at a secesh who ventures too near, but mostly only at a bush or trees moving in the wind or only a few old leaves rustling a little; or anything that appears like a man to whoever is standing guard. And then one is burned past him, then the cry of "Halt!," and if there is still movement then the monster is investigated by the lieutenant or the sergeant with a few men. If it is nothing, then the guard gets his ears chewed and is called a pants-wetter and that is the end of that.

Yesterday I felt so dizzy again, as I often have as a result of too irregular opening. But a half pint of castor oil helped me out of it, and today I feel as well as a fish in water.

Greet everybody heartily from

your Henry

Camp Steele December 6th 62

Dear Mother!

Yesterday already I wanted to reply to your letter, but Joe L[edergerber] had something else in mind. He sent me on detail as commander of the pickets. Actually that is the duty of a captain, but he thought I could carry that out as well as any captain, and which I have now survived. Still, it is very taxing to be on one's guard all night and day, to reconnoiter the immediate surroundings, to think out a little plan of how to welcome the enemy most effectively if he should knock on the door, etc., and all kinds of other little attentions to this one or that one. In no case can anybody sleep, for if anybody should not conduct himself as an officer on the picket watch they will take care of him. This way no surprises will occur, a la Prentiss at Corinth, etc.[25]

There I had by all means a fine little place, and with my 80

---

[25] Kircher referred to the surprise Confederate attack at Shiloh, Apr. 6, 1862, which resulted in the capture of most of Benjamin M. Prentiss's division. The Shiloh battle was fought, in part, for the possession of Corinth, Mississippi.

men I wouldn't have let any more than 10 living secesh through to take those in camp by surprise. It was sort of a narrow pass that we had to watch, and the only way to get to our camp from the land side. The whole shore here, as almost on the whole river from Columbus on, is flooded by the Mississippi nearly every year for about 20–30 miles wide. It is really incredible, but the traces on all the trees show it all too clearly. Here for example the bottom is about 20–25 feet higher than the water level is now on the river. And judging by the trees, last year there was at least 15 feet of water standing in the bottom, so the river here must have risen 35–40 feet. Just think what an enormous amount of water that takes! Now by January or March we probably won't be here any more, or we would have to swim. Of course that wouldn't be anything new; everything has been there.

There are no Hushers living here.[26] There are two houses, one on each side of our camp. One is used by the 29th Wisconsin Infantry, a new regiment. (Whose colonel and major, before we arrived here, went riding outside the picket lines one day and were captured by a couple of Hushers. Their doctor was also along, but he still came out of it with his skin and is here.) The other is used as a hospital, except for one or two rooms where the family still lives.

In the first, a military court holds its sessions. Bert is one of the court. He told me a very nice widow lives there (husband a secesh fallen in battle) with an even nicer daughter with 4 brothers and sisters (2 boys and 2 girls). And every day he leaves half an hour earlier than necessary to have a sociable chat with the family.

I haven't seen very many or any other Hushers. Often a certain Dr. Powels comes here and has a pass, etc. Our dear generals must consider him to be a very good Union man. Lately he even had a pass through the pickets from General Steele and Hassendeubel for 5 barrels of salt.[27] That is indecent. The salt is contraband and is what the secesh are missing most and what they should least have. Where does a man need 5 barrels of salt for himself alone? Dr. Powels is a secesh and spy, nothing else; that is my opinion. I must close, as we're going to drills. More soon. Greet everyone heartily from me.

Your Henry

---

[26] Kircher's reference to southern civilians or guerrillas, probably a corruption of Hoosier.

[27] Colonel Franz Hassendeubel commanded the 17th Missouri Infantry.

Camp Steele, Mi. December 9th 62

Dear Mother!

To continue from the last letter that I ended so hastily because I had to go to drill; we were stuck on the Hushers. As I now heard, the Dr. Powels I was talking about had his house burned down last night; he says by the secesh, but he still has about 150 of 300 Negroes left. Perhaps they know more about it than Dr. P. lets on. Then the beauty on our right has natural black curls, a beautiful complexion, blue eyes and is named Josie Jeffreize. Bert seems to like to associate with Josie quite a bit.

Otherwise we don't know at all whether there are still many farmers or not. They can't be seen at the moment. We don't have any cavalry on this side of the river and therefore can't reconnoiter to see how things are supposed to be. It would really be desirable if Peter Joseph would come back and go into the whole business with a few powerful thunderations; nobody knows as well as he does who is really the cook and who is the boss.

The day before yesterday, an expedition of 10,000 men came back. It had gone to Grenada about 10 days ago (a little town where the railroad runs from Vicksburg north the length of the state, the first place where it is crossed by a branch line), to destroy the bridge there in order to cut off Price's food. But they were too late, as usual; Price had already done it himself. "You won't catch Price asleep."

Now a couple hundred men were sent to the next little village with two little howitzers to flush out a secesh company, but were run out by a command of 12,000 secesh and had to leave one of their cannons in the lurch in their flight, because the path was so bad and swampy. But they were supposed to retrieve it, since the secesh couldn't carry it away either in their haste. So there was bad luck and only bad luck on both sides, but no spilling of blood.[28] It seems that nobody trusted the others closely enough for them to be able to start shooting. You can see that the 12th wasn't there. We

---

[28] Kircher's information on the Grenada Expedition was inaccurate. Alvin P. Hovey led 5,000 infantry, 2,000 cavalry and two sections of artillery from Helena into the interior of Mississippi on November 27. He aimed for Grenada in order to create confusion in the Confederate army, part of which was led by Sterling Price, as Ulysses S. Grant advanced southward from Tennessee and northern Mississippi. The Federals marched to within seven miles of Grenada but did not take the town because it was strongly garrisoned. They skirmished with Rebel units and withdrew upon the receipt of orders from Steele. The high command considered it a success because the Rebels retreated before Grant's advance. OR, vol. 17, pt. 1, 528, 529, 531.

were only 300 men at Bentonville with 2 cannons, and according to the Southern report there were 400 dead and wounded seceshers without losing a man ourselves.[29]

At first, our chief amusement was to chop around the mightiest of the large trees (cottonwoods, hackberries, sycamores, etc., of 5–6–7 feet in diameter) and then to accompany the crash with a quite murderous yelling and whooping as the tree stretched out its battered limbs the long way on the earth. It really reminded us of our 12-pounders at Pea Ridge, for the whole earth shakes for a mile around when such a giant turns a somersault; and then through the whole forest one hears the echo, the crackling of the breaking branches and finally the last hollow sound repeating hundreds of times.

Now times have changed. We have to exercise 2 hours mornings and at noon, and a lot of posting pickets, etc., so that the people have reduced their private amusements to early devotions on a log, eating and sleeping. Couldn't you send me a special map of Mississippi if you get a chance? I have [one of] Missouri [but] I can't use it now.

Letting oneself be captured by the secesh is out now, as there is an order from Washington in which it expressly states that if an officer ventures outside the pickets without being on duty or under orders and is captured by the enemy, he is mustered out, not exchanged and not paid any more. So there is nothing in letting oneself be captured.

Since you have decided to celebrate Christmas in such a modest way I will be able to participate too. And you, dear Mother, will undoubtedly be so good as to consult with the sisters how it would be most appropriate. Willy should have an officer's uniform or another good coat, as you decide. A jacket will look better than a frock coat for such a small officer.

Hetty a pretty, good little dress according to your taste. To all this you will of course have to add Father to my bill, for the accursed paymaster hasn't been here yet. I hope he will come yet before Christmas. And then I will send Father all the money that I get, subtracting my debts here, with the exception of about $50.

---

[29] The glory of Pea Ridge lasted long and tended to color the memory. Kircher's regiment fought with approximately 300 men, but had the support of five rather than two guns on the retreat from Bentonville. The Rebels did not officially report their losses but a tenth of the number Kircher cited would be much more accurate. Sigel's men suffered about the same loss. OR, vol. 8, 210, 228.

I am again quite well since I have been taking at Dr. Junghaus' suggestion, a bitterwood mixed with "something else" daily before breakfast "to keep the bowels open."[30]

There is nothing new at all, at least we don't hear anything. There are newspapers that come, 10¢ each, and usually 8 days old. But something's got to give soon at Fredericksburg, and in general something ought to give everywhere.[31]

Many greetings to everyone from

your Henry

Camp Steele December 16th 1862

Dear Mother!

All morning long I was busy packing and repacking and busy considering what to pack in this or that place. Only now do I find time to let loose with my thoughts as well as my pen.

The terrible order, already discussed so long and so much, has finally come. Like a thunderclap, the 6 wagons went through every regiment. So from now on we will begin to be soldiers: a reasonable number of blankets, a cute little carpet bag and a large stomach to store up provisions for a month. Therefore I have come to the following conclusion; to send everything home that I can do without and then quietly wait for whatever else happens. I will send my blue chest to Mr. Bremermann by Adams Express and he will then be so good as to hold it until you can pick it up.

If you should not receive the key by mail or opportunity then break the chest open, or let Bernard try whether any key in the store will fit it.

Dear Mother, perhaps you can wear the fur shoes over other shoes in the winter, they are warm. I wish you would take good care of the pipe, as George gave it to me.

I had to send back the books, of course, as a shirt or a pair of pants is worth more to me at the moment than half a library.

We will probably march out tomorrow or the next day. Nobody knows where to, probably by steamboat to the South, Dixie or something like Vicksburg, etc. But I can only conjecture; knowing, no, I don't do that at all.

---

[30] Louis H. Junghaus was the 12th Missouri's surgeon.
[31] Following several weeks of inactivity, the eastern armies engaged in battle at Fredericksburg, Virginia, on Dec. 13, 1862.

Now I must see to it that I get the chest across the river.
Therefore adieu for a while, much more soon.

A thousand greetings to everyone.

Your Henry

Camp Steele Mis. Decb. 17th 1862

Dear Mother!

Yesterday I wrote you a few lines in haste and consoled you
with more and more thorough things for today. If the previous letter should fail to arrive I will partially recapitulate, at least about
the chest, etc.

It is addressed to Mr. Bremermann by Army Express, and a
letter by mail with the request to hold the chest in storage until
Uncle or Father has a chance to receive it. I have a receipt from the
express office and [have] declared the value of the box to be $125,
and accordingly can draw this sum, assuming the box would get lost
or be "other than as the receipt says," namely "Army Express! Received Dec. 16th 1862 of Lieut. Kircher a chest said to contain clothing & ch. Value $125.00 addressed to Bremermann & Co. St.
Louis Mo. to be put in charge of Adam's or some other reliable Express, for transportation according to directions, and their receipt
taken, to which faithful care and attention is promised, without assuming risks incident to fire, navigation or a state of war.
(signed J.G. Forman   Express Agent, Army
          B. Pierce   of the South West."

Now this is your "heart's desire," isn't it? I have paid it as far
as Memphis; from there it will probably go to St. Louis by Adam's
Express. Eh bien, everything will be all right.

All in all, although it is unpleasant, the order is quite good, for
we always did have much too much baggage to make quick movements. Besides, the whole war seems to be going more energetically. It is also high time that the secesh find their end so that we
can provide the *Dumb*ocrats a similar fate.[32]

If now there were really a fresh action, Vicksburg could soon
be taken if it were just attacked once with Mother, Country and
Heaven at the same time, so that nothing would remain for the
rascals but to jump in the air and thus make themselves vanish
with pleasure.

---

[32] Democratic candidates, many of them opponents of Lincoln's war effort, had won surpris-
ing gains in the 1862 elections.

The only thing I regret is that our officer's mess or boarding-house probably has to end if the order is strictly carried out, and there is nothing left but for us to eat with the companies. That would be no misfortune, for I did that earlier as a sergeant and will do it just as well as a lieutenant. We always make everything as comfortable and pleasant for ourselves as possible. Now if the most comfortable is very uncomfortable for us, I will still gladly send myself into it because it can't be helped. Besides, we have it significantly better than those who carry their entire possessions around their necks. "By all means, always as gay and happy as possible."

Henry

Immediately in his future lay campaigning that would contrast markedly with Kircher's brilliant splash into battle at Pea Ridge. Almost half of his term of service in the 12th Missouri had passed, but the hardest fighting still lay ahead.

CHAPTER THREE

"The Consequences Are Gruesome"

Nine months after Pea Ridge, Kircher made ready to enter his second battle. In late 1862, the Confederate stronghold of Vicksburg became the major objective of Federal forces in the Mississippi Valley. Ulysses S. Grant put into motion a double approach to the strategic river town. While he advanced southward from northern Mississippi, William T. Sherman took regiments gathered at Memphis by John A. McClernand down the Mississippi to attack Vicksburg from the river. On his way, Sherman planned to pick up the division to which Kircher's regiment belonged. Because Osterhaus had been on a series of sick leaves since late July, Frederick Steele led the division.[1]

Camp Steele Mis. December 18th 1862[2]

Dear Mother!

Because we got our wagons, etc., things seem to be going again today or during the course of the day, as soon as the boat intended for this side arrives (perhaps the *John Warner* again). In any case we can't go right away, since most of the steamboats have few or no cabbages and have to get them from the upper Mississippi (St. Louis, etc.), and therefore it is possible that we will lie around for 3–4 more days.

Besides, we will have to wait for Sherman's or McClernand's (if they would belong with us) troops.

To all appearance you will have to wait for a while with the box of goodies (which certainly would be very nice) until there is a chance to send it with somebody.

You can imagine how difficult it is for me to write today. Just think, if you were going to move from home to another house and you were trying to write a letter amidst all the sliding and lifting, the pushing and the uproar, the bellows of joy, the cursing and the yelling of a few hundred fellows who are acting like a chained dog that has been suddenly unleashed, you can get a rough idea of what a

---

[1] B. H. Liddell Hart, *Sherman: Soldier, Realist, American* (1929; reprint, New York, 1958), 161.

[2] This letter was appended to the letter of Dec. 17.

fix I am in now. Therefore, pardon me if my letter is not as long and understandable as usual.

We are all hale and hearty and are looking forward tremendously to the reception or the Schmiss [dueling scar] that we will get at Vicksburg.

As soon as we are gone on the boat our correspondence will suffer until the right connections are made. It should be 14 days—3 wks. without your getting a letter from me.

A thousand hearty greetings to all!

Your Henry

On Board *Thomas E. Tutt* Decb. 22nd 1862

Dear Mother!

Just in haste, I will report to you that we are finally on the steamboat and we probably will depart today; we don't know where to, but down the river, that's for sure. Yesterday morning about 60–70 ships passed of all kinds and sorts, gunboats, etc., laden with troops, provisions, etc., McClernand's and Sherman's commandos, and today we will join them.

Last night, Capt. [William] Mittmann arrived from St. Louis and reported that there was no thought of Osterhaus's coming. Chaplain [Albert] Kraus hitchhiked to Memphis and had a bunch of letters, perhaps one for me.

Wishing you all a pleasant Christmas?! and myself probably a celebration in Vicksburg, I remain, throwing out a thousand hearty greetings to you,

Your true Henry

Grant's Vicksburg plans went awry almost from the beginning. Confederate cavalry under Earl Van Dorn destroyed the Union supply base at Holly Springs, compelling him to cancel his overland advance. Sherman, however, proceeded with his part of the program. A line of river bluffs, the key to a successful investment of Vicksburg, stretched northward from town. Low, swampy land, traversed by the Yazoo River before it emptied into the Mississippi, lay for miles before the bluffs. Sherman's flotilla steamed up the Yazoo to deposit its cargo of soldiers onto this wet, dismal battlefield. For several days of confused maneuvering and muddy, often vicious fighting, they tried to crack the Vicksburg defenses at one of their strongest points.[3] In a long narrative letter, Kircher vividly described his experiences.

---

[3] Hart, *Sherman,* 161–63.

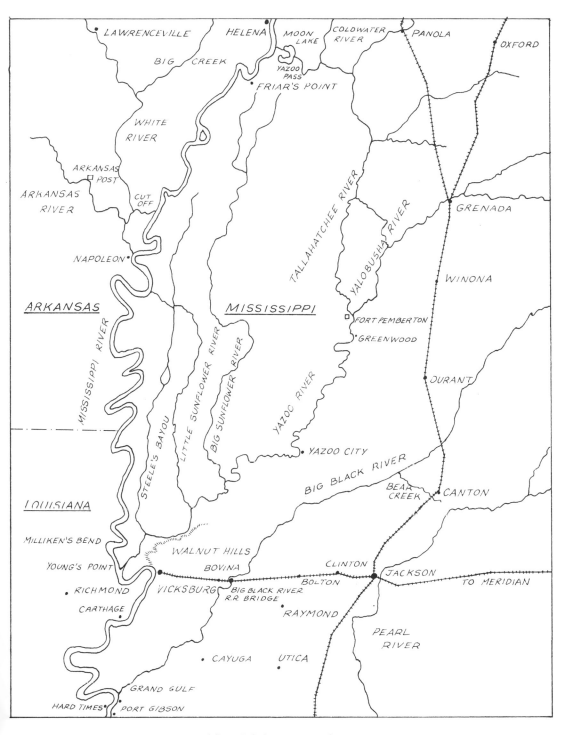

The Vicksburg campaigns

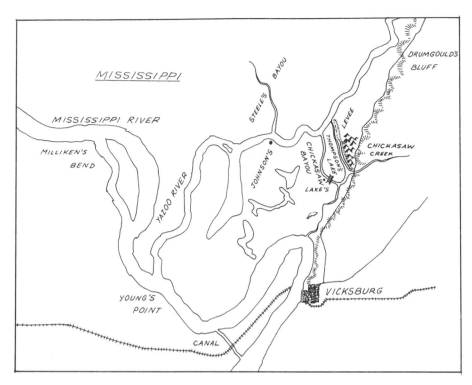

Chickasaw Bluffs

Steamer *Thos. E. Tutt* January 3rd 1863

Dear Mother!

Although I know that I don't have any opportunity now to send you a letter, I still finally took enough time to write one; especially since we mutually, that is the secesh and ourselves, got in each other's hair during the days between Christmas and New Year's.

We left Helena with a troop number of about 25–30,000 men (as I estimate) on 75 steamboats, accompanied by about 15–20 gunboats of all kinds, altogether about 150 guns small and large on board. And also we naturally had our field artillery, about 7 batteries (6 cannons to 1 battery) consisting of 12 and 6 pounders.[4]

It must really have been a magnificent and beautiful view to see all the steamboats puffing here and following on the heels of the others. Just as a regiment starts a march—it was, to be sure, a rather long regiment, at least 25–30 miles from first to last. On the

---

[4] Sherman reported approximately 30,000 men and at least fifty-eight transports in his flotilla. *OR*, vol. 17, pt. 1, 602, 614–15.

whole trip nothing special occurred, except at every plantation where prominent secesh lived and felt the desire to pepper into our boats, but nevertheless did no damage. [They] only caused pleasure for many of ours, since every colonel had an order from Genr. Sherman to land immediately as soon as a boat was shot at and next to burn down the houses of the residences from which the shooting came. So it happened that almost all the houses, with the exception of the small towns, were burned down. They generally already stood in flames or lay in ashes when we came past.

So we arrived on December 25, 1862, at 4 o'clock in the afternoon at the mouth of the Yazoo, and threw anchor here during the night. We spent Christmas night like all other evenings, days and hours on the boat; one snored, most played cards, others read or chatted about the past. If one compared this pitiful evening with the preceding ones, which was awaited so beautifully, so desirously with impatience, this talk did not help anything at all. Finally, with great effort and might, so that everybody would not stretch his dwindling purse too extremely and rob it of its last few coinlets, because before Christmas everyone could at least see what his fate in this world was, it was possible to get a bottle of brandy from the bow of the boat. So everybody could greet his distress with a not any too great sip of the noble juice of the grain and in this way to soften his sufferings a little, and you can imagine that the rebels were damned and cursed.

I was the only one who was consoled, for I received a Christmas present, and it was you again who thought of me. The chaplain had given me the 2 pairs of socks and the chocolate the evening before, so I had cause to be more contented than the others, except I would very much have liked to have had a letter from you with pictures of you all in it. I keep thinking the chaplain had a letter for me and that it got lost while he was performing his office and proud duties.

In short, I comforted myself with the hope that there will also be good times sometime again.

If we could only get some news from the North from time to time! Nothing yet since we left Helena, except a Vicksburg paper of December 24 that somebody took as booty from a house when there was a chance, in which there were all kinds of reports complaining about the Yanks and Feds and still scheming.

So after the not very pleasant Christmas evening, we went at about 11:00 A.M. on December 26 a few hours up the Yazoo with

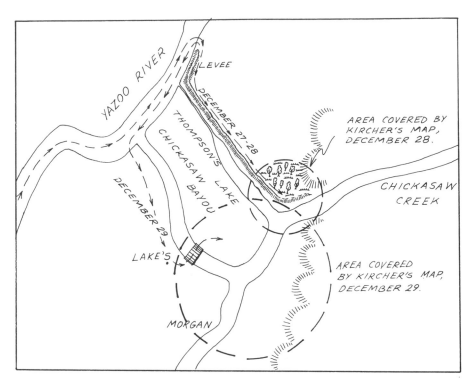

Chickasaw Bayou

the entire fleet. At 2 P.M., we landed on the left shore of the river [at Johnson's Plantation] and heard fairly hefty cannon thunder about 6–8 miles before us. Later, it turned out that the gunboats had shelled the timber. After we unloaded and ate the evening meal, we had the pleasure to bivouac in the open air during a fine and oppressive rain.

I wrapped myself in my rubber blanket and let it rain to its heart's content without getting wet. Others were not so lucky. Why had they neglected to buckle on such a blanket?

The next morning [December 27], we shipped out without wagons etc., back on the *Tutt* and went upstream until 10 o'clock. Here we heard cannon fire again quite near from heavy guns about 2 miles from us. We landed and got positioned in battle lines, impatiently awaiting the moment when the first ball would fly through our ranks.

We didn't have any more to do here, since the lot fell on us to stay with the boats as reserve. Actually, nothing happened that day; there was just marching back and forth to reconnoiter the terrain and the gunboats fired a salvo of bombs from time to time at the hills and into the secesh camp. On the evening of this day we finally got an order to march on downstream toward the levee, which we then quickly completed, as we were very tired of waiting and standing still. After we had gone for about 3–4 miles this way we halted and had permission to stretch our limbs to our heart's content, but not to set any fire because it would give our position away to the enemy. Unfortunately, it got very cold in the night (what one would call cool and fresh in the North) and most of us spent it walking around, since our baggage and tents were, as you know, back at the first landing.[5]

Finally, the long hoped for day [December 28] dawned, for all this time there had been no night for me. The cooks were sent farther back to cook some coffee, which they then brought to us after a long wait. Happy to get something warmer in our bodies, we greedily slurped a significant serving of it with great satisfaction. The day was not yet in its clothing when the word came to get our weapons quickly, and the rest of us were instructed to stand alertly in the woods.

Soon it was "forward" and we advanced about a strong ¼ mile in Column of Divisions, when a swarm of small arms balls showed that the enemy was not far away. But he had shot too early, as the balls came limply and didn't disturb us anymore. Now we deployed and went into "line of battle" until a swamp and waterhole stopped us. Here we lay our bodies comfortably the long way and attempted to spy where, how, when, etc., the enemy was.[6] When one of the [Rebels] shot pretty well and started up almost as if to meet somebody, 3–4 shots were sent that way and the fellow stopped quacking. Now we first realized that it was terribly foggy this morning, and the fellows were well covered by the levee. Since the water did not allow us to be able to chase the fellows away by storm behind

---

[5] Steele left Frank P. Blair's brigade at Johnson's Plantation and took John M. Thayer's and Charles E. Hovey's brigades when he sailed farther up the Yazoo on Dec. 27. The 12th Missouri belonged to Hovey's command. Steele intended to advance along "an old levee" that stretched from the Yazoo to the foot of the bluffs just north of Thompson's Lake. His men cut roads downstream through timber to reach the levee and started on their planned route that evening. Ibid., 606, 651.

[6] Steele's men stopped 800 yards from the bluffs at a bottleneck covered thoroughly by Confederate fire. A short distance beyond, they found a corduroy causeway covered by two enemy batteries with supporting infantry behind the levee, which curved to provide convenient protection for Rebel rifle pits. A "timbered marsh," Kircher's swamp, lay to the left and Chickasaw Creek, Kircher's "waterhole," lay to the right. The Federals stopped in order to feel their way carefully along the exposed levee. Ibid.

the levee, we then had to pull back until we took 2 positions, and one company stayed back to hold the fellows behind the levee in check.

Now our artillery began to chatter lively, but on account of the strong fog they didn't see the fort at all and shot pretty much at

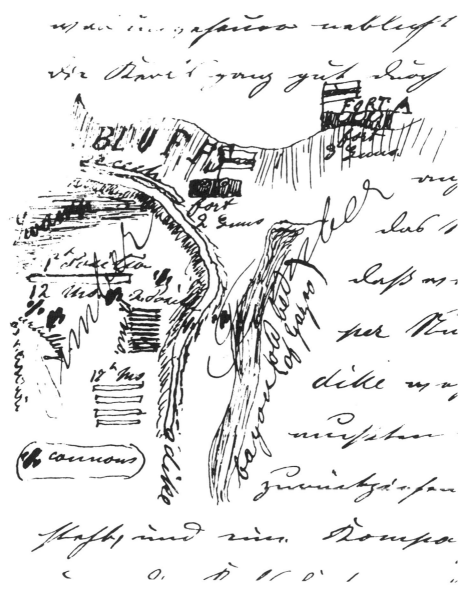

Battle of Chickasaw Bluffs; sketch in a letter dated January 3, 1863, of action on December 28, 1862.

random, only got a reply here and there, but rather more sharp.[7] One could tell that [the Rebels] were not lazy, but had practiced many times and knew how to aim to hit this or that spot. Despite all of that, the balls went mostly over our regiment with grim hissing and whooshing and caused a way of killing time in other regiments farther back. The levee also protected us.

But one hollow ball, indeed it was a lucky shot I think, otherwise a master shot, came just as about 6–8 pioneers were sent ahead to move a tree about 30 steps from us away from the levee and had just gotten to the work. It lay on the tree for a moment in the middle of the small party and then sprang open with an explosion that knocked both legs off one of the pioneers and sent them far apart. It injured another severely on the lower body, who will probably also be dead. It wounded a lieutenant who commanded them and also three or four others less severely. A large piece of the shell about a pound in weight buried itself in the head of Charles Becker, cousin of the one who lost his leg near Pea Ridge. He was immediately dead, as the entire upper head was separated from the lower part. Naturally, he was very disfigured, but still his suffering was short or not at all, for he gave no sound, twitched a muscle; better so than mutilated.[8]

Another shell seemed to take a liking to me, but when it noticed that I didn't care for it struck a mighty oak and rebounded and remained lying a few feet behind me. One of the men was stupid enough to lift it up. I yelled to him to throw it quickly over the levee, since it could still explode. But my protective spirit did not seem wise, and he took out the pin (by which a shell is ignited and explodes); for if it had exploded, there would have been certainly 20–25 dead and wounded, and in any case I would have been one of them.

The whole day went by without much more happening, except that there was a lot of noise and thundering done. But to the right

---

[7] Capt. Clemens Landgraeber's Battery F, 2d Missouri Light Artillery. Ibid., 651.

[8] Steele reported less vividly the party's decimation: "Both [Landgraeber's] battery and the pioneers were subjected to a murderous fire and the pioneers either killed or wounded." Ibid. Charles Becker was a private in Company A. His cousin, also named Charles Becker, was a Company B corporal whose right leg was shattered by an artillery projectile on March 8. Ironically, he received his discharge from the army only three days before his cousin's death on the ill-fated levee. Muster rolls; casualty sheet, undated, Charles Becker service record (Company A): certificate of disability for discharge, Dec. 25, 1862, Charles Becker service record (Company B), NA.

of us, where Generals [George W.] Morgan and Sherman stood, there were more bloody heads. They came close behind one another and we couldn't cross [Thompson's Lake to support them].[9] When in the evening night covered its dark cloak over everything, we were again out of range of the shots of the enemy cannons.

So ended the 28th of December, as we pulled back about a mile to the Yazoo and bivouacked there in the open air. The next day, somewhat refreshed by sleep although somewhat frozen in the process, we went about ¼ mile downstream with the boat (because otherwise we would have had to pass a bayou [Chickasaw] and without putting up a bridge it would have been impossible) and landed, stayed on the shore until 11 A.M. when we received an order to move forward.

We marched to [Lake's] plantation and made a short stop there, when I had time to observe the 10 prisoners that Morgan's command had taken on the previous day. They were clothed ragged enough to be sure, but were healthy, strong, young fellows. Two of them were turncoats and German; besides that there were 3–4 Germans among them and an Italian. One of the turncoats used to work at Mohlmann's; I have forgotten his name. He was immediately recognized by true Bellevillers and not badly dressed down, as he was a secesh, a German and on top of that a Belleviller.

Soon the order was "forward," and we marched "by the flank, right in front" across the bridge of the bayou and took our position as you will see in the drawing.[10] Then Col. Wangelin called us

---

[9] To Steele's right, George W. Morgan's division advanced to the right of Chickasaw Bayou until it was stopped by Chickasaw Creek. To Morgan's right, Morgan L. Smith's division also ran into a bottleneck covered by Confederate fire. To Smith's right, Andrew Jackson Smith's division demonstrated with little effect. When Sherman learned of Steele's failure, he ordered him to support George W. Morgan. The absence of a bridge across Thompson's Lake forced Steele to reembark his men, steam a short distance down the Yazoo beyond Chickasaw Bayou, and follow Morgan's new line of advance over a bridge the latter constructed across the bayou near Lake's plantation. Steele worked all night to ready his command for the move. *OR*, vol. 17, pt. 1, 606–7, 638, 651.

[10] On Dec. 29, Sherman exerted his most strenuous effort to gain the heights. Steele took Thayer's brigade to join Morgan's division and left orders for Hovey to follow as soon as possible. Morgan conducted the main attack that day, sending Blair's brigade of Steele's division and John F. DeCourcy's brigade of his own division forward between Thompson's Lake and Chickasaw Bayou. They lost heavily and were unable to break the enemy lines. Part of Thayer's brigade attacked in order to support them. Hovey arrived just after the assaults ended and took position between Chickasaw Bayou and Thompson's Lake on ground Blair had held before his attack. Morgan also sent part of his division forward to the right of Chickasaw Bayou; it was stopped by a Confederate battery. *OR*, vol. 17, pt. 1, 607–8, 638, 652.

(the officers) to him and told us that our assignment was to take the height, the path, the rifle pits and Fort A, and to secure it, through the brush, the bayou, the swamp, the shrapnel and the balls and whatever kind of resistance we might encounter, forcing our way through. From the place where we were standing to the heights it might have been 6–700 yards, and then just as far to the fort. Therefore, almost a whole mile of double step through all the named cannibals, perhaps even more that were unknown to us; and among those, perhaps hidden ditches on the mountain or hellish machines that would eagerly devour us—who could know?

So that now many a little heart started to beat somewhat faster than usual. I observed the place and saw immediately that if someone was lucky enough to slip under all the bullets, when he arrives on top, he will be greeted most courteously with a bayonet and is no more. So I shortly decided, after the colonel dismissed us, to offer a bold front to the enemy. I saw all of you standing before me as if alive and wrote down everything in my notebook.

Now I waited for the word "forward" and believed that I would shortly have done my last service for my Fatherland and be transformed in the hereafter above. You can imagine that this was a painful half hour for many. I noticed various faces that almost visibly changed and got paler and paler. The eyes looked so hollow and as if they were fixed in the head. And the hands gripped the rifles crowned with the unmatched weapon, the knife, and believed that they had found their own rescuer in that. Others looked terribly solemn and seemed impatient for the moment when they could sacrifice themselves. Still others, and so was it with me, were determined, pressed their lips together and stared at our flag, which was going into battle for the first time and perhaps the last time. But the look was not only sorrowful, although one saw the past expressed in it, but also fiery, serious, showed decisiveness and all muscles swelled mightily to test all the strength that one can offer the enemy to defend one's life to the utmost. But with all this I had the feeling that nothing could happen to me, although I saw the cliff before me and nobody would easily come through alive.[11]

Thus went about a good half hour. I had looked at the watch; it was 4:30 P.M. Now it suddenly began to rain and we got the order to go back about 400 yards into the woods and about 5:00 it

---

[11] Steele described it differently: "Hovey's brigade" waited for "orders to storm the enemy's position, which his whole command, I am told, was anxious to do." Ibid., 652.

was black as pitch. We spent the night here in the rain without fire, tent, coffee and with a blanket.

Nothing came of the storming, since [Frank P.] Blair was here with his commandos and had already attempted the storm. Most of them didn't advance very far at all before they turned around, except the 58th Ohio (which sacrificed about 300 men dead and wounded as well as their brave Lieut. Col. Dister, who commanded it, and all the officers but 3 were wounded or killed) and the 13th Illinois, which left their Col. Wyman and likewise about 200–300 men dead and wounded on the battlefield. All these data are not yet certain; I have just heard, so wait until I can give you the Official Report.[12]

It was complete madness of Sherman to think of such a thing, not even knowing the terrain, for a part of Blair's Brigade was also sent there where the arrow is pointing before the 17th Missouri, so they wouldn't have gotten there at all, just us and the 76th Ohio.[13] Therefore he would have just sacrificed us all, because Mr. Sherman believed that he could take Vicksburg with such a handful of men before Grant or Banks would think of it.[14] Then he would be the great hero; not those, those really courageous and brave soldiers who happily looked into the jaws of death and went into the gaping jaws, and it pleases such a simpleton to say "forward." I am convinced that 200,000 men wouldn't take the forts from that side, for they could hardly climb the hill even if there were no enemy there. Our guardian angel has once more taken the 12th under his wings.

From the drawing, you can see how each fort guards the oth-

---

[12] The 58th Ohio lost 111 men, including 11 officers killed and wounded. The 13th Illinois lost 163 men. Peter Dister was killed that day and John B. Wyman lost his life on Dec. 28. Ibid., 656–57.

[13] The 12th Missouri was scheduled to repeat Blair's heroic but disastrous attack. Chickasaw Creek, to its front, was 100 yards wide. Quicksand covered its bottom and a stream fifteen feet wide and three feet deep also lay within its banks. Those banks were ten feet high and crowned with felled trees entangled with their stumps to form a network designed to trip up anyone who attempted to cross. In addition, extensive Rebel fortifications covered every angle of approach. As Blair put it, the obstacles demanded "almost superhuman efforts." The route Kircher marked on his map for the 17th Missouri apparently had been taken before by most of Thayer's brigade in an attempt to support Blair. The route was a mistake that took four of Thayer's five regiments out of action. In short, Hovey's brigade probably would have repeated Blair's and Thayer's high losses and lack of success. Ibid., 652, 655, 658.

[14] Nathaniel P. Banks advanced northward from New Orleans with a large force. His objective became Port Hudson, Louisiana, the only other strongpoint on the Mississippi in Confederate hands.

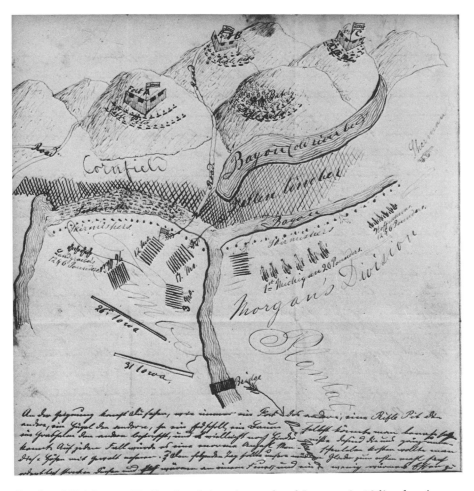

Battle of Chickasaw Bluffs; sketch in a letter dated January 3, 1863, of action on
December 29, 1862.

ers, each rifle pit guards the others, each hill guards the others; one
could almost say one blade of grass protects the others, and there
may even be difficulties there that are totally unknown to us. At
any rate, it would take an enormous number of human lives if one
wanted to take these heights with force.

On the following day [December 30], our tired limbs were
permitted to stretch for the first time and to warm themselves by a
fire and to consume a little warm food. (This day, only after the
second day, was a Flag of Truce sent to the battlefield to pick up the
dead and even still many wounded from Blair's troops. We heard
the poor people often, whining and calling during that time, and
couldn't give them any help since the enemy kept up a murderous

fire at those who attempted to rush with assistance to those suffering.) They, the secesh, didn't help them either. They just went around during the night and pulled the boots and trousers from the dead. Of course we couldn't fire at them when we heard them for fear of hitting one of our own men. On this, the 30th of December, there were still 200 some bodies of our brave ones gotten and buried under the cover of a Flag of Truce. It is nothing to see a battle, but the consequences are gruesome.

Now the thickest crumbs were still lifted up on New Year's night. On the evening of December 31, we had to unload all our rifles. No loaded rifle was allowed in the 4th, Steele's, our division, which, it seemed, had received a quite special and unique task.[15] As soon as it was dark, we marched silently back to the landing and shipped out with 2 more regiments on the *Empress*, and rested on the other side of the river and waited for whatever plan would be forged now. At 12 o'clock at night, Col. Wangelin called the officers of the 12th together and showed us the plan. There are 6 gun and mortar boats altogether, which in an hour and a half will throw *only* 14,000 rounds, shells, etc., of not any too small caliber into and around the various forts. As soon as this occurs, we land with all possible speed and storm the forts as quickly as possible with bayonets, stick everybody down; but not a single shot shall occur, for that could foil the whole plan.

After Col. W. had given us this New Year's wish, we went back into the cabin and brooded about what was going to become of us if we would make that many bayonet charges. But it got to be 2:00, 3, 4, 5; the day dawned and we still didn't hear any cannon shots. We were about 3 miles below the gunboats and it would certainly have been the most magnificent fireworks and New Year's shooting that the world had yet experienced. Just consider, 14,000 booms in an hour and a half! That is over 155 shells in a minute. It is enormous. I would have liked to see and to hear this. One paltry 12-pounder almost bellowed me deaf on the first day of the man-

---

[15] Unable to break through the Rebel center, Sherman planned to try the enemy's far right. Several miles up the Yazoo, Drumgould's Bluff extended to the riverbank. If the fortifications could be taken there, Sherman could gain high ground without forcing his men across the swampy terrain that had helped defeat his earlier efforts. Steele's division and the First Brigade of Morgan L. Smith's division boarded boats that night and steamed to Drumgould's. Admiral David D. Porter's gunboats were scheduled to silence the Rebel artillery before the infantry attacked. *OR*, vol. 17, pt. 1, 609.

hunt here. What kind of *agitation* that would be for my ears! That would be *critical. Nott for a Million* (as our chaplain would say).

Well it didn't happen, and New Year's day I spent in the middle of a battle for the first time without hearing a shot.[16] In the morning, we were set on land opposite our old place and got orders to make ourselves as comfortable as possible. Nobody had to repeat this to us. Soon a hearty fire was burning and the sun was also more merciful than in the last few days and shone friendly on us as if it was glad that a new year had come in.

I was rattled out of a deep little sleep and a steaming noon meal spread a splendid aroma. You can imagine that everything smelled splendid, even if it was only salt pork soup, beans, pork, hominy, tongue and coffee. But if one hasn't slept right for 5 days and eats always in great excitement and nothing but a little bread and coffee here and there and a little bacon, one forgets the urge just to ask for raisins. I still had a bar of chocolate, even so, and I thought "You must still wait a little as long as there is anything else," and so it happened that I still found it in my pocket yesterday (Jan. 3rd) and consumed it after I had previously totally forgotten it.

After a second nap, I was awakened again and there was a fragrant bucket filled with quite genuine fusel (in Belleville, people call it whiskey) for the officers. Naturally the men had their portion too, and so we celebrated the new year in satisfaction with song and tin cup clanging and a half pint of rot gut at the forts before Vicksburg without having taken them.

At 4 o'clock [January 1], we went back on the *Empress* and at 12 at night we landed a few miles below at our old *Thos. E. Tutt*, boarded it and pulled out the next midday [January 2] at 11 o'clock with long faces.[17] At 6 o'clock in the evening we lay at Milliken's Bend and today, the 4th of January, 1863, we left there and are now underway farther north; where to is unknown, but in general we

---

[16] The assault had been planned for 4 A.M., Jan. 1, but was cancelled due to dense fog that immobilized the boats. Sherman "was sadly disappointed," but admitted that even if the landing had been successful, Steele's assault "would have been attended with a fearful sacrifice of life." Ibid.

[17] Considering the stout defenses, the appearance of Confederate reinforcements and the low bottomland subject to flooding if the Yazoo rose, Sherman "saw no good reason for remaining in so unenviable a place any longer." His men reembarked by dawn, Jan. 2, and steamed down the Yazoo and up the Mississippi to Milliken's Bend. Ibid., 609–10.

will have to do with only unknown great things from now on. The enclosed violet is from a plantation near Milliken's Bend where we loaded fence rails. I think the owner's name was Burns.

I must praise our chaplain, by the way, as he ministered to the wounded very much, continuously helped bandage them, amputate, etc. He stated that he had experienced more in the 2 days when so many wounded arrived than in his entire previous life. He looked very exhausted and tired and complained so about the American doctors because they were always drinking schnapps and didn't give him any.

Where we are going God knows, or perhaps only our generals and the enemy, but we certainly don't.

McClernand came here on the 2d with his staff, but not early enough to tone down Sherman in his first madness. I believe the fellow is obsessed with storming or himself is always in a storm. Although I don't know much about McClernand, I still trust him more than Sherman.

I wish we had our Franz [Sigel] and our Peter Joseph again. Since Peter Joseph (Osterhaus) isn't here, General [Charles E.] Hovey commands our brigade. By God, that is a model of a general, a piece of furniture. If we hadn't had Hassendeubel with us, who predigested everything for him that he had to do, he would still be standing there like a cat roars at mice.[18]

He came to one of the men standing picket and placed himself there like a child who has——in his pants. A sentinel called to him: "Fellow, old fellow, to what regiment do you belong?" "Why, I am General Hovey." "You General Hovey? Any damn fool might say he was a General."

January 7. Yesterday, General Osterhaus, B[ill] Wangelin and Capt. [Christian] Andel came here, 50 miles below Napoleon. The cards and 2 letters from Capt. Andel, the chest with goodies to eat from Bill Wangelin [arrived] together with a letter; you can imagine that my joy was not small to receive a letter from you again, the first one since the 8th of December. The pipe from Uncle came very desired since I had lost my previous one in camp on the Yazoo River, and a man without smoking apparatus is really not one.

---

18 Kircher's remark about the German-born Hassendeubel contains overtones of ethnic prejudice, for there is no evidence that Hovey performed badly. Steele seemed satisfied with his brigadier's work throughout the campaign. Ibid., 651.

Now I have almost completely wrung out my heart for this time once again. A thousand greetings to all.

Your Henry

Sherman's Chickasaw Bluffs Campaign ended in frustration and defeat. When McClernand joined the expedition, he took command of the land forces and looked for further action. Obviously, Vicksburg could not be taken easily but another Confederate river point appeared more vulnerable. On January 4, McClernand set his command out on the "unknown great thing," as Kircher put it, which developed into a full-scale expedition to capture Arkansas Post and its Fort Hindman. Situated thirty miles up the Arkansas, the Post provided a haven for Rebel boats that occasionally annoyed Federal river traffic on the Mississippi. To secure uninterrupted communications and to give the men something to do, McClernand decided to snuff it out.[19]

Fort Hebert near Arkansas Post[20]
January 13 1863

Dear Mother!

As it seems, I only get a chance to let you hear from me when I have something significant to tell you. We fought a battle again and were victorious; not like at Vicksburg, retreating with long faces, but quartered in the (for soldiers) comfortably furnished log houses in the rear of the fort in great numbers in rank and file, standing around just as friendly to take us in as they protected their makers, the secesh. But they were not impregnable. At least they let our weapons of death in.

In order to make the thing more understandable, I will start from the beginning. On the morning of the 9th at 10 o'clock, our fleet, transports, gunboats, etc., went up the White River to a canal that leads to the Arkansas River, on through it and about 20–30 miles more up the Arkansas. It was evening; we landed and the troops all got on dry land to be placed in battle lines. Then a "stack arms" was made; we cooked and, as we like to say, "slept on our weapons." To be sure, I lay on my blanket and covered myself with my sable. During the night, our evil spirit made terrific attempts to drench us thoroughly. But despite all his rumbling he was only able to scratch a few drops out of the clouds, which by no means were able to cause a pause in our snoring.

---

19 Hart, *Sherman,* 166.
20 Kircher insisted on referring to the fort as Hebert.

The next morning, that is the 10th of January, a general labyrinth of troops, wagon parts, horses, donkeys, and everything possible began to form, until each regiment was provided with 4 wagons and 5 days of rations. Then the various divisions, brigades, regiments, and batteries were sent into motion to find their places in the line.

At 7 A.M., the gunboats began sending out hollow or other balls where the so-called Fort Hebert was supposed to be. They got no reply until finally one of the gunboats got tired of all the waiting and swam quite nonchalantly upstream to quite close to the fort and gave it a broadside which it seemed to feel, because it awakened out of its rest and thereupon cut loose too. I couldn't see any more since we had to march into the woods behind the fort, where we didn't see anything more of the boats but heard all the more of their cannons.

We spent the whole day in running around and boredom. In the evening, our regiment was called back to guard a road where the enemy could wait for reinforcements.[21]

On the 11th, the cannons began early to roar quite merrily: sometimes stronger, sometimes less strong. But about 2 P.M. we heard our gunboats getting louder and louder, until about 4:00 they had roared themselves into such a frenzy that it only seemed that everything was one incessant roll of terrible thunder; just here and there getting softer for a moment, but only to emphasize the next one and make it all the louder.

At 4:30, everything got still. This seemed quite peculiar when suddenly, after such a racket that seemed to make the earth cave in, there was a sudden stillness. Soon there came the news that explained everything. The enemy had hoisted the white flag, had surrendered.

The following morning [January 12] we finally got the order and permission to leave our tiresome post and report to the fort. That was an accursed assignment, to lie down for the duration and

---

[21] The troops landed at Notrib's Plantation a few miles downriver from Fort Hindman on Jan. 9. The next day, Steele's division tried to find its way to a point on the river above the fort. The "old wood road" Steele followed took him across a bayou and in a roundabout direction. The division retraced its steps to the landing and prepared to spend the night. Before it bedded down, orders arrived for Steele to march again along a more direct route. Hovey reported that he left Kircher's regiment at the landing to guard the transports. By the morning of Jan. 11, Steele had his division in place on the extreme Federal right, facing a line of Rebel fortifications extending inland from Fort Hindman. *OR*, vol. 17, pt. 1, 754, 765–66.

hear all the cannonading and shooting and not participate. But somebody had to guard the position and it was our lot.

Now I can tell you what I had later heard and seen. There were not many dead. Individual regiments may have suffered fairly hard but only because of stupidity. When they had already stormed the rifle pits they turned around and exposed their backs to the enemy for a short time and, not being lazy, the enemy peppered them hard.[22]

You will probably get to see the Official Report before I do. Our booty consists of 4–5,000 prisoners, 23 guns and also field artillery, a mass of weapons of all kinds and all transportation. Besides that, 2 more regiments of reinforcements came to occupy the fort, whom we genially requested to just put down their weapons and consider themselves prisoners of war, which they did. At noon today, they and the other prisoners departed to be transported to Cairo or someplace else.[23]

All the other acquaintances and relatives from Belleville in the 12th are safe and sound, as we are. We have marching orders again to get out of our secesh block houses and onto the boats to leave again; where to, I don't know.

I got a Belleville newspaper today but no letters. It is strange. They must have probably been on the *Blue Wing*, which the secesh took at the mouth of the White River, towed it here and burned it down after they had looted it.[24] More soon, I have to break off now. As soon as we are on the boat I might get time to write more. A thousand greetings to all.

Your son Henry

The capture of Arkansas Post was as successful as the attacks on Chickasaw Bluffs proved futile. But the brilliance of McClernand's victory did not make it more important strategically. Vicksburg remained the most vital link in Confederate control of the Mississippi. After leveling Fort Hindman

---

[22] Hovey's regiments suffered heavily. Two assaults were made: one with the 76th Ohio and 25th Iowa, the other with the 3d Missouri and 31st Iowa. Both failed; the Ohio unit lost 68 men and the 3d Missouri lost 75. Kircher's "accursed assignment" possibly saved his regiment needless casualties. Ibid., 716, 718, 766.

[23] McClernand reported capturing 5,000 prisoners, seventeen large and small guns, 3,000 small arms and much other material. He forwarded the prisoners to St. Louis. Ibid., 708.

[24] A detachment from Arkansas Post had captured the *Blue Wing* and its cargo of ammunition a few days before the Post fell. McClernand used the incident as partial justification for the campaign. Ibid., 709.

and burning the log houses, McClernand's soldiers made their way back to the river above that stronghold.[25]

Board Steamer *Thos E. Tutt* January 19th 1863

Dear Mother!

Now we are on the way to Vicksburg for the second time and will probably still arrive today at Milliken's Bend. I wonder if we'll be more successful this time. It is possible that our army is strengthened by about 20,000 men plus two generals in whom I have great trust. Also, a fresh gunboat has made its appearance with us. It is a kind of *Monitor* armed with two 15-inch Dahlgren's leeches.[26]

It is really remarkable and unbelievable; however, I have seen it and am convinced. Of two 100-pounders standing in casemates by the fort (Arkansas Post, which we took), one of the same was pierced in the middle by a cannonball. In other words, 7 or 8 inch thick cast iron was penetrated like a feather. The other was hit on the mouth so that its upper lip dissolved and the whole cannon made a backwards somersault. The casemates still bear many traces of balls. The former consisted of a log house in which the walls as well as the roof were made of 3-foot thick wood faces. Along the front there was a 6-foot thick end wall and the roof was also covered with railroad rails. But the [projectiles] were so effective on the roof and against the sides that they broke through the iron rails a great deal as well as the wooden walls, and probably also delivered the secesh cannoneers quite unpleasant boxes on the ears.[27]

But enough of this. Our gunboats have proven that they are extraordinary machines for destruction and death. If only our "old Abe" had a few more gunboats.

Jan. 22nd. Now we lie again at Milliken's Bend. Whether we stay here for long or whether we perhaps advance right away to camp, that the gods know, or probably only our generals. It is reported that we went into camp here until the transports have gone back and brought Grant's Army Corps here too, so that we can then make a common attack. Others claim to know that we went here in the country to join with Banks on land.

[25] Hart, *Sherman*, 169. Diary, Jan. 13–14, 1863.

[26] Kircher's "two generals" probably referred to McClernand and Osterhaus. The latter rejoined the army just before the reduction of Arkansas Post but took command of a different division. Grant's troops, however, had not yet joined McClernand. *OR*, vol. 24, pt. 1, 10. The "fresh gunboat" probably was the *Chillicothe*.

[27] For graphic illustrations of the worsted casemates, see *ibid.*, vol. 17, pt. 1, 714–15.

But all this is just told so much and speculated until it finally reaches from many to a majority. The news in the newspapers usually originates this way. In any case Vicksburg will become the Richmond, or the cupping glass, of the West. Now come what may, I am willing to wade through thick and thin in blood up to my knees if thereby the last Negro and the last traitor finds his death. Whenever this is completed I too, as we all are, am ready to set the head straight on "John Bull or any other man."

Now, there are found here among the Hushers quite a few of the opinion that the South would be ready to join the Union right away, to uphold the old laws and to bear the costs of the war *jointly*. I replied to them that if all that would happen and in a few years the South had stolen all the weapons, etc., the dance would start anew. They shrugged their shoulders and said they didn't think so.

If our Linc. would only hold the Gray a little stiffer, pray less and guide more, and garnish the halls more with secesh and traitors than with our own people, as in an order that went out from Washington signed by the President. It states that a teamster shall suffer death from hanging because he shot a Negro, a rather special rap on the knuckles. Is a Negro more than our Fatherland? Why aren't fellows other than real soldiers given the scaffold when they are discovered undermining the Union? If 100 of these fellows were decapitated it would be a warning for thousands of others, and at the same time it would spare lives, save them. But the way it was and is being carried on, so many brave and dutiful soldiers who have lived many happy years in the bosom of the old Union find their graves, as well as many villains. But this is now on our old topic, which of course is by far unexhausted. Still, I am disgusted with it.

We get newspapers and letters only seldom or not at all since we started our meanderings on the Mississippi, Arkansas and White rivers. I believe for sure that a half dozen of your letters to me went astray when the secesh took away the *Blue Wing* at the mouth of the White River. Well, if one of their men did get them, he couldn't begin to read them. After all, there is a war in the land. Did you notice it yet?

Soon I will perhaps have more news to tell again, for the numerous gunboats and soldiers can't have come here for no purpose. As I send you and everybody a thousand greetings, I am waiting for the next letters to come soon.

Your true son Henry

The 12th Missouri spent January 22 at Milliken's Bend, then proceeded downriver to a camp within sight of Vicksburg. Grant authorized construction of a canal designed to cut across the neck of land opposite the town. If successful, it could have allowed boats to bypass the Vicksburg defenses.[28]

> In Camp vis-à-vis Vicksburg Jan. 26th 1863
>
> Dear Father!
>
> The little drawing above may serve to give you and all of you a little insight into our present task (taking Vicksburg). Of course, it is very much lacking as far as the position of the enemy camp and batteries go, since up to now we do not know them; we can just see two forts and the one battery. The distance from Vicksburg to the canal in a straight line might be 3½ to 4 miles. From the battery to the mouth of the canal is 2½ at the most. They can often reach us with their cannons when they shoot full balls.
>
> Now, the curve in the Mississippi from one end of the canal to the other is supposed to be 15 miles long. The canal itself is scarcely 2 miles long but 10-12 feet deep, just as wide above. It runs down in the shape of a funnel until it is 2 feet wide and is supposed to be or is now being made 3 feet wider, so that it will be about 15 feet above and 5 feet below. When we arrived here, the water was hardly in the canal. Now it flows 4–5 feet deep in it, but too slowly to make the canal wider and deeper. The current of the river doesn't run directly into the embankment but, as it seems to me, hits about 50 feet above the bank and then rebounds into a dead corner, as shown in the arrow near A. However, this can still be helped by a second small canal that would meet the first one about 20 feet from the beginning.
>
> Another, in my opinion, very clumsy mistake is that the canal is not deep enough before one gets to the quicksand, where then a quite small current takes it away considerably while it takes a significant rapids to wash away such firm yellow clay. If the river is not a secesh, though, it will still rather more comfortably enlarge the canal according to our wishes. Judging by how it rises, it will be on our side in the end. However, if it rises 10 feet more, then everything here will stand under water. The mountain that is about 12 feet high would protect us but only as long as it would cut us off from the enemy and until the river would flow through wildly, embracing us with its irresistable arms until it had made drinkers of

---

[28] Diary, Jan. 22–23, 1863. *OR*, vol. 24, pt. 1, 8.

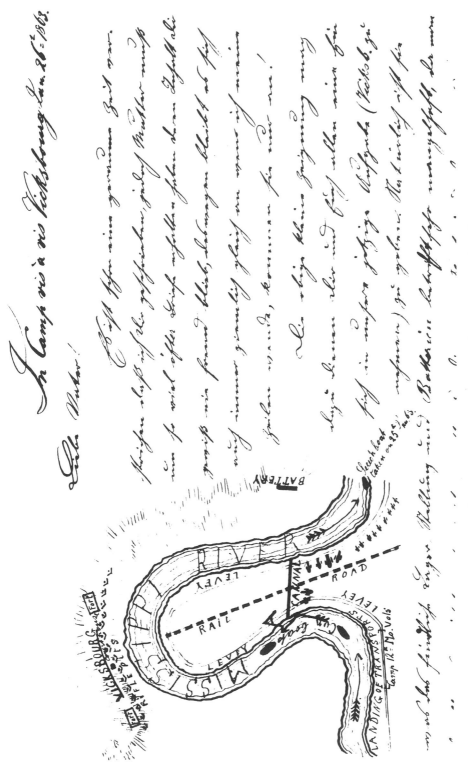

Vicinity of Vicksburg; sketch in a letter dated January 26, 1863.

so many with its caresses and cajolery, and then irretrievably given them the draught in which death is found: in a word, "drownded."

It rains here practically every day for a few hours in the morning. From this the roads are in a miserable condition, and we find ourselves forced to build a complete corduroy road that leads to the mouth of the canal, about 3 miles long. You can imagine what fun I had when I and 30 commandeered men spent the day working on the road yesterday while it rained quite faithfully. But with all kinds of good words, besides very different "God damns" and dirty looks, I succeeded in keeping my men pretty much in the swing until we had completed about 300 feet of road after half a day's (6 hours') work, and went back to camp. Such tasks are always very unpleasant because one can't teach the men that a soldier occasionally has to work.

The evening of the day before yesterday, a ferry boat was taken by our men while it was landing on this side of the river (see drawing) to take on some wood that was on the shore.[29] A few hours earlier, a steamboat went past our cannons (two 30-pounders and one 20-pounder Parrot gun) without being visibly damaged, although it was fired on 6 times. Our gunners just can't shoot on the run.

I really hope the paymaster would show up here sometime. There is already quite a little heap since last February, almost a year: over 1,000 dollars. I never had that much before.

Yesterday I received a Belleville paper from the 15th of January; that is, in 10 days. According to it, there is somewhat of an uproar in Illinois. And justifiably so, if it is true that many of the Democrats are impudent enough to make their traitorous comments the way they have done.[30] If they don't get invaded there soon with the sword as well as with the rope I don't know what will happen to our country. No punishment is too hard for a trai-

---

[29] The boat was the *DeSoto,* carrying a supply of eggs, chickens, butter, and sweet potatoes. Members of the 13th Illinois Infantry heard its engine as it approached a woodpile on shore, unaware of the Yankee presence. The Illinoisans hid behind the levee until the boat fastened a rope to a tree and then captured it. *Military History and Reminiscences of the Thirteenth Regiment of Illinois Volunteer Infantry in the Civil War in the United States, 1861-1865* (Chicago, 1892), 296–97.

[30] The Democrats fared well enough in the November, 1862, state elections to control the Illinois legislature. Arthur Charles Cole, *The Era of the Civil War, 1848-1870: The Centennial History of Illinois* (Springfield, 1919), 297. Even before the 23d General Assembly convened on Jan. 5, 1863, rumors circulated in Springfield that the Democrats had already formu-

tor. Whoever asks questions for a long time is evading, going the long way around. We have come to the point where the people have to begin to show who is the master and everybody who opens his mouth against the government gets it closed forever with the hangman's rope. If this had happened from the beginning there would now be peace in the land and there wouldn't have been so many lives lost.

Oh, has it really gone so far that a second revolution is breaking out, and in my home state? Then I would evaporate here and make my appearance with you; not to fold my hands in my lap, no, to establish in the State of Illinois a butcher shop where there is only flesh of traitors to the State of Illinois and the United States. I hope it doesn't go so far, for then I wouldn't stand for all that which I would be capable of doing.

You probably are amazed at such talk from your quiet Henry. Just believe you knew me but now you don't know me anymore, for the experiences that I have collected so far have served to embitter me against all who think otherwise from the way I think, and especially against those who refuse to defend their Fatherland, to strengthen me in body and in the feeling that I felt for every fellow human. In short, I am a different person since the day when Goerge was no longer, except my love for you is the same or even stronger.

Greet everybody heartily

from your son Henry

Camp vis-à-vis Vicksburg January 30th 1863

Dear Mother!

Yesterday, General Grant arrived. His Army Corps is expected here today or tomorrow. He will probably take high command here.[31] Likewise, there are about 200 blacks who arrived to work on the canal. It will take a lot of work to complete it. Besides, the river is already almost equal with the shore here and will soon

---

lated plans to use their new political power to promulgate antiwar views. A newspaper correspondent expressed sentiments that were similar to Kircher's: "Are we on the eve of a revolution in this State? Is Illinois to be plunged into the same condition of war and desolation as Missouri, Kentucky and Tennessee?" Three days later, the Democrats proposed resolutions denouncing the Lincoln administration and the Emancipation Proclamation, and calling for a negotiated settlement of the war. *Chicago Daily Tribune,* Jan. 5, 7, 9, 1863.

[31] Grant assumed command of Union forces before Vicksburg on Jan. 30. *OR,* vol. 24, pt. 1, 11.

drive us out if it rises much more. That would not be so bad at all! Anyway, I have little hope that the canal will be crowned with success. In my last letter to Father, I discussed it adequately. I believe we will spend weeks if not months here without doing much, as long as Banks and Farragut don't make their appearances.[32] They will probably also have to pay a toll at Port Hudson, [Louisiana]; it is supposed to be strongly fortified.

The rebels are also gathering an enormous number of troops together here. They are supposed to be about 60,000 strong in Vicksburg and receiving more men daily. We number about 30–40 thousand.[33] Of these, however, about half are now unfit for service. The passage on the steamboats has damaged almost all of them more or less, for there are no appliances for cooking properly. The men had to live mostly on half-boiled coffee with crackers, together with some raw bacon, from which most of them got diarrhea. If we keep having good weather here now and the people can get situated a little more comfortably, the health of the troops will improve significantly.

Our regiment has held up quite well in comparison with others. At the present we are just as strong, or rather just as weak. Other regiments had 60 and 80 or 100 sick; our highest number was about 30 or 35. Overall, one finds that the regiments consisting mostly of Germans have better health than those consisting of Americans or Irish. First of all, the German stomach is better attuned to sauerkraut and root plants and therefore can stand pretty much everything. Besides, he is no sweet tooth who eats sugar or molasses by the pint. He also cooks the little that he does want nice and well done. We also bake pure flour. There is always good bread in the oven, which [the oven] we make with our fingernails from dirt if there is no stone to be found. And cleanliness is also much more in fashion among the Germans than in the other regiments. This contributes no little amount to good health.

You don't need to pity us because the paymaster went through $200,000, for this small heap would have been no more than a drop in the sea. Just think; there are so many soldiers in the West and what would 1 dollar a man be, where U.S. now owes him for 4 months, for 6 months at $13 per month? So you don't need to feel sorry for us because of one swindler.

---

[32] David G. Farragut led naval forces on the lower Mississippi River.

[33] Grant reported approximately 51,000 men near Vicksburg. *OR*, vol. 24, pt. 3, 20. Confederate strength probably was nearer 30,000 to 40,000.

You mustn't consider me very moody if I ask for my chest again. But I see that the others all have kept their chests and suitcases, etc., quite unhesitatingly. Why shouldn't I too? Besides, everything gets wet for me in my knapsack when it rains. Now, only to help me out of all this, I would like either a good strong valise of leather or rubber. Or just as well, and it would also be less costly, my chest.

I would like my uniform back. However, the books are too good and too heavy to carry around and lose. Otherwise, a few old or ragged magazines would be quite pleasant to kill the time dead with.

Otherwise I don't know of anything at all. A little shoe polish or such knick knacks are always welcome. Tobacco would also not be sneezed at. Everything is enormously expensive here if there is really something to be had, and there is no money at all. We have already tried all kinds of weeds, grapevines, leaves of all kinds, but still haven't found a surrogate for the noble toback.

Probably two weeks will have gone by before this letter reaches you, and I will probably get [the chest] yet in February or in March. Will we still be here then? I think so.

Just write often, even if you aren't clear what we are so piously doing, for that is always hard to say. For, like God's ways, those of our generals are also marvelous.

My hearty greetings to all. More soon.

Your son Henry

CHAPTER FOUR

"The Glorious Yazoo Pass Expedition"

During the winter months of 1863, Grant tried to keep his men busy while waiting for spring and better campaigning weather. He initiated work on several projects, such as the futile canal. Although his confidence in their success was not unqualified, the work took the men out of their crowded camps along the river.

The most ambitious project proved to be the Yazoo Pass Expedition. It involved sending 4,500 troops aboard thirteen transports, accompanied by six light gunboats and two ironclads, on a 600-mile journey to reach the line of bluffs that lay only ten miles from the 12th Missouri's camp. The armada planned to steam up the Mississippi to Helena and enter Moon Lake through a cut in the levee. From there, it could proceed through a cotton canal unused in ten years, the Yazoo Pass, and sail into the Coldwater River. The Coldwater flowed into the Tallahatchie, which joined the Yalobusha to form the Yazoo River. If all went well, the invaders could then clear the same bluffs that had stopped Sherman the previous December and open an avenue for the rest of Grant's army to pour onto the high ground north and east of Vicksburg.[1]

Among those regiments chosen for this bold venture was the 12th Missouri.

> On Board Steamer *Emma*, Miss R.
> February 7th 1863

Dear Mother!

Yesterday afternoon at about 5 o'clock, our regiment and the 17th Missouri (Turner Regiment) boarded the steamboat *Emma* at the landing vis-à-vis Vicksburg and headed upstream the same evening. As far as I can learn, we will enter a bayou or lake on the left bank at Friar's Point, 15 miles south of Helena, which we can travel in high water, as we have now, down the Coldwater River and so get into the Yazoo River without having to pass the various strongly fortified bluffs on the left bank of the Yazoo; which doubtless would be pretty risky and probably somewhat unpleasant for transport. About 40 secesh transports are supposed to have made

---

[1] Bruce Catton, *Grant Moves South* (Boston, 1960), 377–82. Richard S. West, Jr., "Gunboats in the Swamps: The Yazoo Pass Expedition," *Civil War History* 9, no. 2 (1963): 157–58, 160.

their way to the upper part of the Yazoo together with a gunboat (à la *Arkansas*) and one ram waiting there; which we, namely our flotilla, should ambush in their hollow (with our approximately 20 gunboats and rams—mosquitoes, ironclads, and all kinds of other long-legged creatures). We will, depending on the circumstances, either capture or do them in.

As soon as we catch up with the fleet, which left a day earlier because it is slower, our regimenters will be divided among the gunboats at Commodore [David D.] Porter's discretion as sharp-shooters. So far I can't tell you anything more about our expedition because we haven't experienced it yet. "What can't be cured, must be endured!" But we all have great hopes for a good and probably also adventurous, as well as a successful expedition; especially be-cause our party is made up of gunboats, rams and 12s, as well as 17s, which so far have held up well.

The ram *Queen of the West*, whose pleasure trip past Vicks-burg's batteries I described adequately in Loulou's letter,[2] was turned back from a scout down the river after the hero and com-mander of the ram fleet, Col. [Charles R.] Ellet, had sunk 3 secesh transports loaded with provisions and taken 8 rebel officers cap-tive. He set the crew and soldiers of the same on dry land because he didn't have room on his boat, and he and his men turned back safe and sound. He will probably soon be at the head of a second expedition or will strut by Vicksburg again with disdain.[3]

The chief and strongest requirement of us all in the army is to spy the paymaster among us. It is really a pitiable feeling, particu-larly for an officer, to lie around and carry nothing but a 25-cent check on the Belleville Savings Institution in his pocket, which no-body here will accept. The only satisfaction that I can get out of it is to examine it from time to time, give it a good crumpling and then, with a g——— d——— stick it back at its old flank until further order.

---

[2] This letter is not extant but Kircher recorded the event in a diary entry of Feb. 2, noting that the boat absorbed eleven Rebel hits but lost no crew members. On his way past the town, Ellet rammed and set fire to the Rebel *City of Vicksburg* but the Mississippi's current and energetic fire fighters foiled his attempt to destroy it. He reported receiving twelve shots. *OR*, vol. 24, pt. 1, 336.

[3] Kircher's grapevine information was remarkably accurate. Ellet steamed south below the mouth of Red River, and captured three boats and seven officers as well as many civilian passengers. Because they were unable to keep up with the *Queen*, he burned the boats and their cargoes. The civilians were released but the officers were escorted to Northern lines on shore so they would not be exposed to Rebel fire as the *Queen* passed batteries at Warrenton. Ibid., 338.

The main consolation is that nobody has anything and therefore nobody can lend or borrow anything; consequently we are "all
in the same fix."

Our officers' mess is suffering greatly from the Schwindsucht
[disappearing disease] and is getting thinner every day. Uncle Sam
has a curious setup for his officers. We can only actually get provisions from him for cash money; and now where are we supposed to
get this? So far we have still found a sympathetic individual here
and there who is willing to lend us something on our honest faces
and shoulder straps, even if it was only Swiss cheese the last time,
with pickles and dried herrings. Still, that's something.

It seems to me, according to the newspapers, that it would be
time for a certain class of Democrats, namely in the State of Illinois, to wear a hempen necklace. The fellows are really too brazen,
the miserable, underhanded traitors. Isn't there anyone left in the
whole state who will give a scoundrel such as Richardson a blue
ribbon to swallow? Oh, it is time for the Republicans to come
home and hiss the "Broom rangers" off the stage! Would that it
were with bullets! What shall this all become anyway? A terrible
blood bath, or an even more miserable peace?[4]

Whenever I uncover a newspaper here and there, I only see
more and more new miseries that are constantly occurring in our
land. Of course, they are merely short paragraphs and only serve to
bewilder one more; but there is always enough scandalous news in
them that if I think about that and what still is to come my head
only roars, and I regret that I am not capable of more, not even as
much as many. If not, may the devil fetch me if it doesn't appear
otherwise from here. I am very pleased that the French got a scar
on their face in Mexico! If they would leave other people in peace,
they wouldn't burn their tongues.[5]

The boat is shaking so much that it is hard to write. Au revoir.

Your true son Henry

Board Steamer *Emma* Feb. 10th 1863

Dear Mother!

Since the opportunity arises so favorably, I will grace your eyes

---

[4] "A bitter opponent of the [Lincoln] administration," William A. Richardson was elected by
the Democratic Illinois General Assembly to fill the U.S. Senate seat left vacant by the death
of Stephen A. Douglas. Arthur Charles Cole, *The Era of the Civil War, 1848–1870: The
Centennial History of Illinois* (Springfield, 1919), 298.
[5] Napoleon III's attempt to establish French power in Mexico was going awry.

with another scrawl, since you will read it anyway because it is from "your Henry."

The night before last we suddenly felt a terrible crash. Casimir Andel, my roommate, and I almost flew out of our beds. My first act was to go to the upper deck to find out the cause, which soon proved to be that we were not going any farther because a sandbar prevented any progress. All the efforts and measures of the captain of the boat seemed to be in vain. The boat sat still and just wagged its tail here and there as if quite content with its master, but there was nothing further that could be done. Very bad ink!!!! The signal for help was given out into the world but there was no answer, although the *Skylark* (a boat) passed by where it could clearly see. She probably thought the rebels had us cowering and therefore puffed away as fast and as mightily as possible instead of coming to our aid, as a decent ship's captain would have done, come what may.

Finally around midnight we perceived a second, increased, improved, reproduced and reinforced edition of a crash, so that the whole ship trembled from stem to stern and groaned and moaned. Then we saw the smoke and steam from a steamboat and discovered that the former secesh ram *General Bragg* was offering its help in this manner by ramming us.

The kick in the seat of the boat had helped us, although by chance it had happened in the dark of the night, and it made us navigable again. Only it also tore out the entire starboard stern guard; but the rudder for steering remained undamaged for some inexplicable reason and could be used some more.

It was really amusing to get that bump all at once without knowing the cause, although we were all standing in the rear of the ship in order to make the front as light as possible. But the guy came so fast and soft creeping up to us that nobody knew. Well, everything turned out happily and the whole story has to be regarded as a good joke.

By the way, the enemy would have had a fabulous opportunity to do guerrilla fighting, for we could only have gone into the puffs of air without finding our destination or any protection.

I believe we will stay here for one or two days until the passage in the Yazoo is finished and we can move forward. Many pilots are of the opinion that it is impossible for us to go down there with the big gunboats. We will find out!

A thousand hearty greetings to all.

Your son Henry

Board Steamer *Emma* at Helena, Ark.
February 17th 1863

Dear Mother!

I just learned that we will be paid tomorrow and since there will be important news then in any case, I decided to wait one more day with my letter.

February 18th. As stated, we were paid this morning up to the end of October. My portion of the festivities comes to the trifling amount of $850.10. You can hardly imagine what a pleasure that was for a shrinking pocketbook, as mine was.

I intend to send Father $300 which should be used as follows, as long as Father and you all have no objections. First, Mother, Sophie [a sister], Loulou, Josephine each $10. Second, Willie, Henriette, and Virgie [a nephew] each $5. Third, to go towards a gravestone according to your taste for our dear George's cool bed, $50. Total $105. Perhaps the remaining $195 will hardly cover my debt at Goedeking and Kircher's but it will pretty much make it, and I can probably send the rest soon, since the paymaster told me we would probably be paid in 2 or 3 weeks for 2 more months. But that isn't quite so certain and I must hold some so that I don't get such a bad mood in my pocketbook again. The money, or rather the beer, put the people in such a good mood that it has become a young hell on the quiet *Emma*, and writing a letter is quite some assignment.

[William] Bliesner, a sutler, will probably go to St. Louis in a few days to get some wares and will then get my blue chest or whatever you want to send. You mustn't forget to put the key in an envelope so that he can show the contents to the provost marshalls, etc., if it is required, since the sutlers are always kept pretty much under their thumbs on account of the various kinds of schnapps and wine, etc., that are so softly packed in sauerkraut or innocent cheap cigars (stinkadores). It is kind of a custom of sutlers, Jews, Yankees and *the like* (whoever that may be) to smuggle, and they are quite inexhaustible in such kinds of invention.

About that which one must think of when one gets up in the morning until going to sleep, and maybe even half the night, the whole day long and always, immediately and continuously, without seeing any light of improvement, joy or any other pleasant thing; namely, our unhappy land. I will not say much if possible, for I only get upset and can only complain about the whole swindle. And our correspondence shouldn't become like newspapers, sheets of smears and lies.

This much is certain; that the sun will come up and go down for severererererel more times before peace is again produced! Oh, if I could only swallow 100 secesh and 200 Peace Democrats each day; I could digest them if they would get down first. I am just relying on Uncle Yates's watchful eye in our Sucker State.[6] If only once in a while a few thousand ropes were set up to make a trap to tie up the beasts as soon as their hour tolls, for it will soon toll. The knotting that announces the strokes is already rattling lustily and may the pen not delay, may the strokes follow many and hard. And if the Union should go down in defeat, may their bloodstains serve as evidence that once a great and rich nation lived, reveled, slept, bled and died here. May their memorial stand high above all others of the same kind; indeed, even in death shall it proudly stand with scorn for all other nations in the world.

In my opinion, we will probably lie here for another 8–10 days and then go to Vicksburg again without achieving our goal, since the river has already fallen 5–6 feet and is still falling continuously. So there can be no thought of going to the Yazoo through the Yazoo Pass, Coldwater and Tallahatchie, since there is still not enough navigable water in the various rivers. But where we will actually get through is hard to say, and it wouldn't matter anyway. We are quite comfortable and well on the boat and now we have money as well, my darling, what else do you want?

A few days ago, there was a comical conversation that occurred here. When we had arrived here in Helena and a great number of officers, among them Col. Wangelin, were sitting on the starboard side devoting themselves to conversation, reading, etc., there suddenly appeared a young man, ruddy, fat, blond, with pinched-together little eyes, a circular slit on a clock face similar to a full moon, high hunting boots, leather breeches, a brown coat, a stand-up collar and a McClellan cap. And he opened up his feeding instrument and let the following words flow out of it:

Sch. I have the honor of speaking to Col. Wangelin? (with various scraping and bowing).

Col. Yes, that's my name.

Sch. My name is Schultze. No doubt you received the letter of recommendation from General X (a Prussian general who had been to military school with Col. W.). I heard of your regiment and immediately set out to find it to seek a position with it as officer—

---

6 Richard Yates, governor of Illinois from 1860 through 1864, strongly supported the Union war effort.

Col. Hugo Aurelius von Wangelin.

Col. I cannot accept.

Sch. Well, yes, yes, of course, yes. I was an ensign in the Prussian Army and just arrived in the country 3 months ago. I was in the East and spoke with General Siegel and he advised me to enter your regiment.

Col. If you want to enter my regiment as a private that is fine, but I can make you no promises. Everybody is master of his own fate.

Sch. Well, of course, I will probably enter as a private and then soon become an officer.

Col. It depends entirely on you, how you conduct yourself.

Sch. Well then I can enter as a private?

Col. Yes.

Sch. Then I will get my trunk—
Col. Trunk?
Sch. No, no, just a small chest—
Col. Chest?
Sch. Oh, I can pack it all in a knapsack.
Col. Now you can join, but I make no promises.
Sch. Yes, sir, Colonel.

Well now, soon the fool came with his chest and is a private in Company K, my company. I don't know how he will like it. So far he has only brought a fair bit of impudence to light. He's out in the world either because he is a boor who was chased out or some kind of adventurer. If he gets too close to me I'll rap him on the knuckles.[7]

Besides my uniform you could put 2–3 dozen turned down paper collars, No. 15, also a few books to read, but nothing valuable for they get lost and worn out.

Many thousand hearty greetings to everybody from
your true son Henry

Board Steamer *Emma* Helena Arks. Feb. 20th 1863

Dear Father!

Finally, I had the pleasure of being paid. And I would have had almost $200 more since the paymaster thought I was a cavalry officer on account of my large boots and figured my salary on that basis. It caught his attention that I was refiguring and he did the same and said, "Well, Lieut., ah shall be obliged to bring that amount down about 200 dollars." Now I see that he was correct and was very satisfied, for he also paid me as a lieutenant for the 19 days that I was acting. What more could I ask? Now I have paid off my debts here and have about $125 left over. In addition, I have about $150 outstanding from various officers who will pay me next payday. I always have kept and will keep in the future my accounts all in a book so that if something should happen to me you can easily put things in order.

It is already getting noticeably boring lying here on the boat for us. There is also nothing in Helena but knee-deep mud that one can hardly wade through, so there is no question of going for a

---

[7] Thilo Schultze enrolled as a private in Company K on Feb. 13 and served his entire enlistment period. Whether or not he was a boor or an adventurer, he managed to secure detached duty as a draftsman at Osterhaus's division headquarters in April, 1864. Muster rolls, Thilo Schultze service record, NA.

walk. Every day it's the day after tomorrow our expedition goes down the Yazoo Pass, but it just remains at that, and we could stay lounging here for weeks yet.

Many hearty greetings to all.

Your obedient son Henry

The way was opened to the waiting soldiers by late February. On the twenty-second, Kircher's regiment transferred from the damaged *Emma* to the *Key West No. 2* and steamed toward Friar's Point. Two days later, after stealing into Moon Lake, the 12th Missouri was distributed aboard the gunboats as sharpshooters. The expedition started on February 25 and the soldiers turned marines were assigned their battle stations; the tedious advance began.[8]

Board Gunboat *Romeo* River Coldwater, March 1st 63

Dear Mother!

It may be possible that this letter reaches you or maybe not; but better to make the attempt than wait any longer, for weeks will probably go by before there is an opportunity that presents itself to me.

We have a very, very boring (tiring) journey in a narrow channel or bayou about 25–30 yards wide with large trees on both sides, which our ship steadily comes into contact with and very frequently it leaves a piece of roof or porch, etc., on them. Since the 24th of last month, we traveled from Moon Lake by Friar's Point into the canal, and in those 4–5 days we didn't advance more than 15 miles. You can imagine how slowly ship traffic goes in the canal. The Coldwater is not much better and in it we have to go 40 miles to get to the Tallahatchie, then another 100 miles, roughly, to Yazoo City, where the brawl will probably begin. In any case there will be a hot battle: where there will be a victor?

Our expedition consists of 2 ironclads and 6 mosquitos (gunboats) of which the *Romeo* has us, Company A, and Company D as sharpshooters on board. Besides, there are transports with 5,000 troops. On the last day of our lying around I came to Company D as commander, as their captain was placed under arrest, or I would have had to stay back on the transports, which would have been unpleasant.[9] Lt. Col. Kaercher, Capt. Affleck, Lieut. [Casimir] Andel,

---

[8] Diary, Feb. 22, 24, 25, 1863.

[9] Adam Ranft was captain of Company D but his service record mentions no arrest. Perhaps he was one of the seventy-seven regimenters left at the 12th Missouri camp near Grant's

Lieut. [Henry] Seipel [of Company D] and I are here with our companies on board. The officers on the gunboat are very friendly and decent men and we officers all Bellevillers, consequently also decent fellows, and we have very good times.

So far nothing has happened but exercising with our rifles and the cannons, of which we have six 24-pounders, which are manned in part by our men since the crew is weak and consists mostly of young 16–17-year-old lads. I feel sorry for the poor fellows, how they tire themselves out and still don't get anything accomplished from lack of strength.

Many thousand greetings to all. May God protect you all from everything.

Your Henry

Board Gunboat *Romeo*
Coldwater River, March 2nd 1863

Dear Mother!

I just learned that several who didn't find room on the gunboats are going back to Helena, and in order not to miss any opportunity I am writing again.

Now we are only 20 miles from Helena and have to lie here today all day, since the river, or rather creek, is blocked with felled trees. It will be a tedious journey. I wonder if it will pay off. Everybody in the boats is very exhausted, since so many pieces get stuck on the trees.

There was a report here that the *Queen of the West* and the *Indianola* had been captured. I don't believe it. Col. Ellet won't let himself be captured so easily.[10]

I wish the rebels would rebel out, or if I am going to be a soldier my livelong days I would at least like to know it and could then easily adjust to my fate. But when I think what I should do and how should I begin to make myself useful in civilian life, my mind half stands still or it just goes around in my head. Well, I'll just have to take the proverb as my guide: Kommt Zeit, Komm Rath [all things come to him who waits].

---

canal when the expedition sailed for Helena. Muster rolls, Adam Ranft service record; muster rolls, Compiled Service Records of Volunteer Union Soldiers Who Served in Organizations from the State of Missouri, Rolls 487–495, Microcopy No. 405, NA.

[10] The *Queen of the West* was taken in an engagement on Feb. 14, apparently through sabotage by its pilot. Ellet, however, escaped. Ten days later, the Rebels used it to capture the *Indianola*. OR, vol. 24, pt. 1, 18–19, 342–43.

We are all healthy and alert and terribly eager for battle, only I, like most, don't like the idea of fighting side-by-side with a Negro. That's asking a little too much. If the colored and others do government work, I don't have anything against it. But to see him fighting with weapons in his hand at my better side, hey now, no sirree bob. If we 20,000,000 whites can't force, stamp out not even 10 million rebels, then we don't deserve any better than to be ruled by them, amen.

My heartiest greetings to you all.

Your true Henry

Board Gunboat *Romeo*
Junction of Tallahatchie & Yalobusha March 10th 1863
Dear Mother!

Now we have been traveling on the various rivers, bayous and narrow passes for almost 3 weeks, and have gotten to see nothing of either civilization or the world of foe or friend. One can almost hardly describe how crooked the rivers are here; they consist of nothing but rounded corners. At this time of flood one sees shore seldom or not at all, just here and there a little edge of a plantation sticking out. Otherwise everything is forest, sky and water, and quite often just forest and water above and below; but we are under cover and don't bother much with it.

Travel here is really tied with much hardship since the rivers are all so narrow; or better, because the trees standing in the water on both sides of the river hardly permit any turns without running into them, which happens rather frequently. Then a piece of deck or X number of shreds from the *Romeo* usually also stay stuck on the tree. One could apply the saying: Wo die Fetzen hangen, sind die Schiffe durchgegangen [where the shreds withdrew, the ships got through]. The *Carl*, a dispatch boat, just got through and will probably go back to Helena tomorrow, and then there will perhaps be an opportunity for this letter.

We live here on the gunboat quite content. If we didn't know that some time things have got to break loose you might think that we were making a pleasure trip or a voyage of discovery. We, the officers, eat with the others from the gunboat quite famously in a mess and have two of the sailors, the ship's drummer, a jolly lad of 13 or 14 years, and my gentleman of color, Louis, to wait on us. You should see what happens when something is wrong, like yesterday evening for example. There was a broken cylinder on the lamp and it wouldn't burn brightly. Then it went as follows:

Officer: John (the little drummer), why don't you put a new cylinder on the lamp?

John: There are no more, sir.

Officer: If you don't have this lamp fixed up in a decent way in 3 minutes I will put you in the hold in double irons.

John: Yes, sir, but there are—

Officer: Hurry up, go on.

In 3 minutes the lamp came like new born, with a new cylinder and everything. Where it came from, the new cylinder, that is known to the gods. But when there is the threat of the double irons, the hold and bread and water, anything is possible. It may be little pleasure to have one's hands and feet locked in iron sitting in a stifling, cellar-like hole with nothing for nourishment but some crackers and water. I often feel sorry for the poor fellows. They are often only 15–18 years old and naturally more suited for bad jokes than for work, and therefore must frequently do what they like even less, do time in the hold. Well, we've got to keep order, and on a ship even stronger discipline than elsewhere.

According to what the Negroes said on the plantation we just passed we are still about 10 miles from Greenwood and about 100 miles away from Yazoo City. At Greenwood there is supposed to be a battery. Well, we'll find out tomorrow. If it isn't situated considerably higher than the land we have seen so far everything must be flooded there. But Yazoo City is supposedly strongly fortified. If the rebels don't have any good gunboats or rams we will probably take care of them. If they are well provided with them then we will quite probably be defeated, for there is no talk of going past. Here we can't just purse our lips; we also have to whistle. If they capture us they will have to withstand a hot battle and will probably get only the crew of the boats. The boats will probably devour enough fire early enough that they won't fall into the greedy rebels' hands. But one mustn't give up hope; everything will go well.

The *Queen of the West* was supposedly really captured, as they say here. It was a little too much ventured by Col. Ellet to saunter around all alone in an enemy land. But I would have preferred to have set it on fire rather than let it fall into the enemy's hands. But the *Indianola*, I can't believe it. Was it really taken too?

The canal at Vicksburg will probably take years yet before it is navigable, and if it does get that far the bluffs opposite the mouth are just as easy to fortify and then nothing much would be gained altogether. Why didn't we occupy Vicksburg instead of Helena last June and July when there was no danger? There is nothing to blame but the stupidity of our generals for the fact that the South is not farther advanced in its defeat. If we had just half as many generals and they were real generals, real patriots and not speculators and cowardly, conceited sleepyheads! Half a dozen Siegels and Rosecrans's at the head of our armies and the war would be at an end inside a few months. Various Butlers would also not be anything to sneeze at. In short, people who want something sensible and who do it.[11]

But what good does my chatter do? We have been in agreement for a long time about that and can't change it anyway.

I am very curious what kind of new courts the new congress will convene, garnished with Democracy, whenever it meets, which will occur fairly soon.[12] They will probably work very hard to lighten the lives of their Southern brethren a little. Pay heed when peace offers are made to the South. They will slip out of the rope and believe that the page has turned and that they are capable of subjugating the North. Who knows what kinds of thieving and murderous hells will be made of our magnificent land next?

At least this much is certain; that things look very sad for the South, at least everywhere that I have been. Most of the farms and plantations are under water, neglected and cultivated either not at all or very little. In the North, however, everything is going along the old way and one shouldn't believe at all that a few times 100,000 men are standing opposite each other, just waiting for the command to mow each other down. I tell you we can speak of luck as long as the war rages entirely or mostly in an enemy's land.

Now in one sense that is good; the rebel must finally find out that waging war is no child's play but costs house and home and, yes, often lives. If we had only been allowed to begin to rage at will in the enemy land with united fire and sword right away and not been fascinated so much by the Southern brethren.

---

[11] William S. Rosecrans commanded the Federals in a successful defensive battle at Stone's River, near Murfreesboro, Tennessee, the previous December and January. Benjamin F. Butler gained fame and notoriety in 1862 as commander of occupation forces at New Orleans.
[12] Kircher referred to the 38th U.S. Congress, in which the Democrats had made substantial gains in the 1862 elections. The Senate met in special session from Mar. 4 through 14, 1863.

In general, all the people are quite well and satisfied with the life here. The only thing they don't like is during rainy weather to go on a mortar boat to row. During good weather there are always volunteers enough. There is only a 13-inch mortar on it but the mortar weighs 19,000–20,000 pounds and takes from 18 to 28 pounds of powder per load. It fires a bomb of 225 pounds. I'd like to hear it roar once; it must play a lot of music and even more pieces when the ball hits. On our gunboat *Romeo* we have 6 Dahlgrens, brass 24-pounders, and therefore can't really complain about too little noise when the day comes.

Send me in your next letter at your first opportunity some postage stamps. The letters don't go for free.

I am fit as a fiddle and curious what the end of our expedition will be. A thousand hearty greetings to all, large and small, if they are good Union people.

Your loyal son Henry

[P.S.] We have attacked the fort at the confluence of the Tallahatchie and Yalobusha into the Yazoo today, the 16th of March, at 12 o'clock. You will find out how it turns out soon enough. The enemy shoots well and has 4 cannons and about 3,000 men. We won't get out of their fire until we have brought the battery to silence.

The fighting Kircher reported summarily in his postscript was part of a days-long struggle with the first serious Rebel resistance the expedition encountered. At a sharp bend of the Tallahatchie, near its junction with the Yalobusha, Confederate troops had thrown together a fortification made of mud and cotton bales. Fort Pemberton stood on low ground and was completely surrounded by water, its defenses aided by a line of supporting earthworks and a raft anchored in the Tallahatchie. Holding only three guns, it nevertheless proved a resilient roadblock to the armada. Only the gunboats in the van could be used to test its strength and their maneuverability was curtailed by the Tallahatchie's narrow width. On March 11, the *Chillicothe* steamed forward to reconnoiter.[13]

Board Gunboat *Romeo* at the
Junction of Tallahatchie & Yalobusha March 17th 1863
Dear Mother!

So now our experience before Fort Pemberton. On the morning of the 12th at about 10 o'clock, we arrived here and heard that

---

13 West, "Gunboats in the Swamps," 160, 162.

the *Chillicothe* had already traded a few shots with the enemy battery and lost 4 dead and 10 wounded from a single shell that went right into one of the portholes, exploded, and showered the whole crew of one cannon with a rain of iron. Whether and what the enemy lost we don't know.[14] In the night, two men of the *Chillicothe* deserted. They probably went over to the enemy. I wouldn't know where else they would go in this wilderness. I wouldn't want the enemy to have shot or hanged them, for if they should fall into our hands again surely nothing would happen to them.

The next day (the 13th of March) it was "all quiet on the Tallahatchie." There was just reconnaissance and one battery was set up in the woods to the right of the river, consisting of two 32-pound Parrot guns pointed toward the enemy and covered with cotton bales. The day before yesterday, another cannon from the *Baron De Kalb* was added to the battery.[15] Our battery is separated from the enemy by a bayou (a bay) and can't be waded through by the infantry, therefore it's as plain as your hand that the infantry can't do a thing. From the drawing, you can get an idea of where we are.

Now on the 13th at 10 A.M., the *Chillicothe* was first sent forward (an ironclad) and had hardly come around the bend where she is shown in the drawing when she blasted her 11-inchers at the fort. She got an immediate response and started to carry on a jolly conversation with our battery. The *Baron De Kalb* was showing signs of getting impatient and the giant finally began to move slowly and laboriously downstream. It scarcely arrived at the *Chillicothe*'s weak side when it screamed a thundering "Hello!" with 3 firemouths at once, and spat out three 10-inch shells into the face of the enemy. Now it has been thundering for a quarter hour already and we have seen many a ball hit with a terrible force and hiss and bounce off the 3½-inch thick iron tower of the *Chillicothe* and fall powerless into the water or onto the ground.

(At 12 o'clock the *Chillicothe* went back) and we heard our old friend (for we had to bring it here) croak in its deep bass voice so that the whole area quivered; namely with a 13-inch mortar that

[14] The *Chillicothe* made two advances toward the fort and received several shots. One projectile entered a gun embrasure, killed four and wounded twelve men. The Rebels reported no losses. *OR*, vol. 24, pt. 1, 395, 416.

[15] Official reports listed two 30-pounders and one 12-pounder in the battery. Ibid., 395. Kircher's account of the fighting on Mar. 13 compares accurately with the official report.

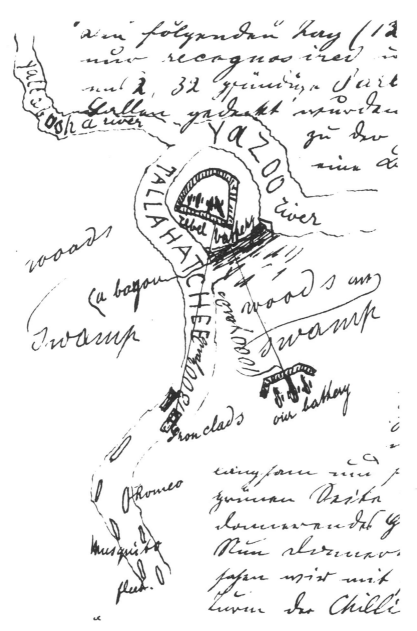

Vicinity of Fort Pemberton; sketch in a letter dated March 17, 1863.

catapults a ball three or four miles when it has been first fed full of powder. However, as I heard, none of the 50 balls that it spat out during the booming fell closer than 100 yards to the enemy in the water in front of the fort. They may have exploded but did no damage except to the pocketbook of Uncle Sam, which got 15–20 dollars smaller with every word the mortar spoke.

The rolling of cannon thunder, the echo of the same, the hissing of one, the howling of the second, the explosion of the third ball all continued without ceasing until midday. We went to eat and enjoyed our meal while the music sounded. This necessary and important business was hardly concluded when we took our former places again in front on the ship's deck, where one could see everything that our gunboats were doing. Now we saw the *Chillicothe* come back slowly, as the cotton bales that we had put on the sides of the tower were all in bright flames and the water that was being squirted on it didn't help to put it out. Therefore it came back to get the men on the mortar boat to help as well in putting out the fire. Just on its return it got the 34th ball, that went through the starboard wheelhouse and two men [were hit by] a few pieces of wood as it whizzed past, one through the arm, the other flung into his face. But both were only flesh wounds, therefore quite mild, considering. The gunboat had not suffered any damage, since most of the balls hit the cotton or the tower and only left dents. The cotton was thrown overboard and the ironclad was all right again. But it didn't go back into the fray anymore.[16]

The *Baron De Kalb* was also called back and so the thunder ceased by and by, and at 3 P.M. everything was so quiet and still that nobody could have imagined that there had ever been anything other than the deepest peace there. The *Baron De Kalb* only received 3 balls, which killed just one man but didn't do any damage to the ship. In the battery, it didn't cost any blood, just powder and shot. Whether the enemy suffered many casualties or not we don't know. However it is suspected, and I myself believe, that we would have taken the fort that day if our ironclads had advanced far enough to send pistol shots into their hides, for their entire fort was smoking and burning, since it consists of cotton and dirt. There seemed to be only 1 or 2 cannons answering. Why we stopped just at the point when victory was most assured I don't know.[17]

---

[16] The boat had been hit about twenty times, according to ibid. One of the two men wounded by splinters was Sgt. Leopold Trost of Company C, 12th Missouri. The injury cost him his right eye. Muster roll; casualty sheet, undated, Leopold Trost service record, NA.

[17] The fire was caused by an 11-inch *Chillicothe* shell that landed among some cartridges. The shell did not explode but its fuse set the cartridges ablaze, burning sixteen Rebels. Another shell wounded three other Confederate gunners that day; one died later. *OR*, vol. 24, pt. 1, 416.

On the 14th and 15th everything was quiet, our generals and Commodore Watson Smith, etc., kept forging plans and throwing them away quickly. Finally on the 16th at 11 A.M., the *Chillicothe* reconvened the party and immediately swam buoyantly downstream. But here it ran into a hot reception right away and had to turn back, as she got a shot on one of the doors of the portholes while they were in the process of loading and it was closed, but was bent such by the force of the ball that it couldn't be gotten open. So nothing became of that day either, since it took a full day's work to set the door straight again.[18]

The wooden gunboats, such as ours, had all taken from 400–500 infantrymen on board. As soon as the cannons of the enemy had been stilled, we were supposed to land at the fort as soon as possible and subdue whoever resisted. Of course nothing came of that, just because a single shot had nailed the door shut and the cannons behind it were no longer usable for the moment. The enemy had also let loose a previously unused cannon, namely an 80-pounder. Once again, through waiting nothing was won! That day we had no loss of life, just one man lost his right hand from a cannon ball at the battery. Just as he was dipping water to keep the cotton bales wet, the pail, water and hand all fell in the puddle and the ball went singing on its way.

Your loyal son

With little else to do but watch the ironclads attempt to reduce Fort Pemberton, Kircher found much time to think about the war and write home.

Romeo, Tallahatchie March 18th 63

Dear Everybody!

Spring seems to be coming on strong, as the sun is burning according to form, the birds are pleasantly chatty, the forest seems to be curtained with a magnificent green veil with a colorful pattern. Everything, everything seems friendly, lively and happy to have the

---

[18] Lt. Cmdr. Watson Smith led the expedition's naval forces until replaced by Lt. Cmdr. James P. Foster on Mar. 18. Gen. Leonard F. Ross commanded the troops. He had arranged for an amphibious infantry assault following a bombardment, but both of the *Chillicothe's* gun embrasures were closed in the manner Kircher described. The infantry remained aboard their boats. The *Chillicothe* lost one crew member wounded and a man at the land battery lost an arm. Ibid., 396.

cold, nasty winter behind it. But not the people, the pitiable creatures—they scuffle, quarrel, murder and plunder in winter and in summer, in autumn and in spring. The beautification in nature seems not to arouse really good thoughts in mankind; continual hate, strife, envy and dissatisfaction are what man always find in it. How can it be otherwise? How else would people who live in such a great, spacious and rich land get involved in such a terrible conflict as the one that has been raging for almost two full years among us, so many liberated from all the sufferings of this earth, but also so many and numerous torn from their pleasures (the few and meager ones of this world), and those pleasures turned into pains.

But what good is all my philosophizing? I can't change all of humanity, and that would have to happen first before it can be different here. Therefore it is better that each one adjust and be satisfied with himself and his fellow man, even if all the rest are indifferent to me. You, my loved ones at home, are still dear and honored to me. It is peculiar, but very often, particularly on days like today, such thoughts come to me when the sun is shining so friendly and everything seems so enlivened. Then I am the saddest at heart because I have to spend the finest years of my youth with such boredom and inactivity. But I know it can't be changed. As long as there is war in the land I will have to play soldier. If I only see a purpose that is really being pursued and that would really be legitimate, then I would allow it to suit me.

The only newspaper that I saw here I bought from a paper carrier for 25¢. It was the *Missouri Republican* of the 7th of March. It had various things in it but only enough to lead one more and more into the dark. Must close. A thousand greetings to everyone from

your Henry

On March 20, the expedition's leaders decided to give up. They ordered a retreat and started back up the tortuous river but met reinforcements on the way.[19] Deciding to make one more try, they turned the boats around. Again, Kircher and his men could do little but watch and listen.

Gunboat *Romeo* Tallahatchie River
March 24th 1863

---

[19] Diary, Mar. 20, 1863.

Dear Mother!

Last Friday [March 20] at 7 A.M., we took an order to go upstream, which we and the entire fleet did. Saturday evening, after
we had put about 125 miles behind us, about 10 transports met us
loaded with troops, artillery and mouth supplies. They came from
Helena, commanded by Genr. [Isaac F.] Quinby, with the order to
turn around and pay the fort a second visit, which also occurred.

Everything went quite well. Since we were the first going upstream we were now the last of the boats going downstream. Nothing special happened until about 75 miles above the mouth of this
river, where the plantation of the rebel Captain Sturdyvant is. We
lay about a half mile below during the night and here we learned of
this captain's abode. Then Bert wanted to pay him a little visit at 3
A.M. At that time Bert with 8 men, under the direction of a Negro
guide, were on their way. They came to a point about ¼ mile from
the house, where a bayou is. They wanted to ferry across it in a canoe made from a tree trunk. They were hardly halfway when the
canoe capsized and its precious cargo, Bert with four of the soldiers
and the Negro, were entrusted to the water, which received them
with open arms. But our heroes began to get uncomfortable and
they crept, one after the other, back onto Terra firma. Now they
were considerably cooled off and returned with long faces and
dripping uniforms to the boat to let the secesh rest.

We decided now that there must be rest! By day we laid on
next to the house, and since we did not find the "old man" we said
to the woman "your most obedient servants." All the chickens,
geese and turkeys were taken prisoner and some were immediately
sentenced to death and the rest are still incarcerated and are awaiting their fates. Naturally, we considered the whole thing a good
joke and continued on without further happenings until yesterday
evening.

Suddenly on the left bank, out of the woods and the canebrake,
there was a jolly bang and a crash onto our iron plates. We saw
about a dozen copperbottoms behind the trees fire at us. The steam
engines were stopped right away and allowed to run backwards, but
we were going so fast that the ship flew about another 600 yards
forward. We turned around quickly, as we only have cannons in
front and on the side, went upstream and fired about 8 or 9 shots
of grape and shells into the woods where we had spied the bushwhackers. Whether it just gave them a fright or also a few bullets
in the body they know best. I only know that it cost enough powder

and lead on both sides and that it rattled enough, at least without causing us any damage.[20]

This morning at 6, Bert and I were frightened to the marrow and the bones, awakened from our dreams by the urgent, on a gunboat, cry of "Fire." Of course we got up a little more quickly than usual in order not to be burnt up in our sleep and investigated. We found that there was no shortage of water where the fire was and soon the former was the victor, eagerly devouring its opponent, who was gasping for air; in short, the fire was put out. Some cotton bales in the engine room had been set on fire through careless handling of a lamp. No damages done.

No longer frightened by this fright, I went to wash and get dressed. At 6:30, just a half hour later, Bert came to me and brought the sad news that one of his men, Henry Schaffner, had just been torn overboard by a branch and had drowned. Despite a boat's being sent after him and our turning around, we couldn't save him. He was seen only once, holding onto a branch. He let loose of it or it broke, and he tried to reach a tree that was only 5–6 paces away from him; but he didn't succeed, for we never saw him again despite all our searching. He couldn't swim at all or we would have been able to save him, for there were several bushes and trees in the water right where he drowned. I feel very sorry for him. He was a good and fine man whom everybody liked. As his letters show, namely one which Father must have written for Schuchmann to Schaffner (according to the handwriting) it makes his tragedy all the more sad, as two of his brothers are perhaps now in Belleville at Schuchmann's and were looking forward to seeing their brother soon. According to his letters and book, he has some money at Romeis' Savings Institution, etc., outstanding. Here we found only the letters, book and articles of clothing, but people say that he had about $70–$80 on him. Bert has already written a letter to Romeis listing everything that his family might want.

At 8 this morning we arrived here again, that is 2 miles above the rebel fort. I wonder what kind of plans are being made? Just now the boat *Alone* has arrived with two 24-pound siege guns. The *Kalne* will undoubtedly soon arrive with 2 such shooting sticks. I don't think we will get away from here before the beginning of May, in my opinion.

---

[20] According to Kircher's diary, this skirmish occurred on Mar. 23, the day after the expedition started back toward Fort Pemberton.

There are about 10,000 troops here in camp as well as two ironclads and 4–6 mosquito gunboats, a few batteries of field guns, some cavalry and Generals Quinby, Ross, [Clinton B.] Fisk, [Frederick] Salomon and Mrs. Fisk, who is acting like "a big swell" with naval and other officers. I always think too many cooks spoil the broth. Now we must wait and see what happens; let's hope for the best! "Poland is not yet lost!" If only there was a real draft!

March 27. Yesterday, the 24th Indiana regiment narrowly escaped being ambushed and taken prisoner. The regiment was reconnoitering on the left bank of the Tallahatchie close to the rebel fort. It also made its way as far as the Yalobusha without any further difficulties except morass and mud, arriving at a field there when a Negro (free American of African descent) suddenly came running toward the colonel and breathlessly called "Massa! Massa! Dey flank you, Rebel flank you ova da!" The colonel looked in that direction and saw that 3 steamboats were landing to their backs. They had to make as hasty a withdrawal as possible in order not to be ground up by 3 rebel regiments. They succeeded in escaping. Ten minutes later the 3 regiments would have obtained their objective. So the Negroes are good for something. The Black will probably soon become a major general, as he already knows what flanking is.[21]

We found the last news in the paper of the 12th of this month. They cost only 25 cents here and go like "hot cakes" or "punch ether." According to the newspaper, the North (the Democrats) is finally gradually coming to reason and realizing that the South will come to its senses only with some decent defeats, and it's high time. Now if only "honest old Abe" carries out the new conscript plan, a few of them will get acquainted with the rope. A thousand hearty greetings to all.

Your loyal Henry

By early April, hope for the expedition's success disappeared. The *Romeo* began its upriver course toward Helena on the fourth, and the next day Kircher witnessed "a very effecting and sade scene," one whose common occurrence failed to lessen its poignancy. "It was a famly of the parents and several children seting aside with there beding and furniture sadly looking on the heap of smoking ashes, formerly their dwelling, which had been put

---

[21] No official reference to this incident can be found, but the 24th Indiana had disembarked on Mar. 23 to reconnoiter. Edwin C. Bearss, *Decision in Mississippi* (Jackson, Miss., 1962), 203.

in the present state by some of the troops in advance, because some guerrillas had probable fired into our boats when passing that plantation. But why do the rebels carry on the war like savages, indians[;] it is but the just punishment for such warfare. They will not gain by it, a plantation and it's crop is worth more to them than 30 lives of our brave men, although to my Knolledge they have Killed but 4 of our men in such warfare during our occupation of the river, and they lost several plantation. When will they learn to meet their enamy in open field?"[22]

Board Steamer *Romeo*
Coldwater R. April 7th 1863

Dear Mother!

We will hardly arrive in Helena before Friday, although we have only 30–40 miles still to put behind us in order to reach the Father of all Waters.

The fact that L. Hauck's office was plundered will make every reasonable man more happy than sad, for if someone can't work any better with letters of the alphabet he doesn't need any.[23] He ought to thank God that the B[elleville] soldiers aren't back home yet, or parchment would have long since been made of him (it is made out of donkey's skin, you know). Those who have such big mouths behind our backs now had better have themselves "iron clad," because the after-effects will yet come in the form of many thrashings. He who laughs last, laughs best. The jug will only go so long to water until it breaks, and then whatever is in it will drown.

Henry Schaffner's body was found 8 days after his drowning and buried. He was fished up by some of Quinby's regimenters and so we didn't get to see him. According to the description and what he had on him, we are certain that it was him. It was said that he had a pretty large wound from a blow over his right eye. This must have been from the branch that sent him overboard, which probably knocked him unconscious right away and therefore he was just plain helpless. So far, Affleck has not succeeded in getting the effects found on H.S.'s body. Who knows whether he will get them, as the fellows show no desire at all to give them up, for there are always no-goods. Somebody may have perhaps gotten into the things.

April 9. We just arrived safe and sound in Moon Lake and by noon we will be in Helena. The captain of the *Romeo* says we will

---

[22] Diary, Apr. 4, 5, 1863.
[23] Louis Hauck, a Democrat, was editor of the *Wochentliches Belleviller Volksblatt.*

remain there only a short time and then go straight to Vicksburg, where the glorious Yazoo Pass Expedition will come to its conclusion. Many hearty greetings to everybody and more!

Your son Henry

The *Romeo* stayed at Helena only two days while the rest of the expedition pulled itself out of the river network into the spacious Mississippi. Kircher and Affleck made a beeline for town as soon as possible, where they found enough lager beer "to make [their] faces smile for 6 weeks after taken." They reached Young's Point on the evening of the twelfth and disembarked the next day to march to the regimental camp. In his wet home, Kircher sat down to provide a detailed travelogue for his home folk.[24]

Camp at Young's Point near
Vicksburg April 15th 1863

Dear Parents!

The most unpleasant part of the whole expedition was on the last day, the unloading and marching into camp during a rain splashing not so very softly on the ground. Well, we were initiated by it right away into the disagreeableness of soldier life again and reaccustomed to it. Since you write me Mother that you haven't heard anything more from us except that the smokestacks of the *Romeo* fell over, it will be best if I deliver you a little description of the expedition.

On February 24, 1863, after traveling on the steamer *Emma* to Moon Lake from Vicksburg, we went on the various mosquito gunboats that were lying there. Onto each of the waiting boats there came 2 companies, either from the 12th or the 17th Missouri regiments, as sharpshooters. The expedition started its long march on the 25th, as one ship after the other disappeared into the bushes on the southern end of Moon Lake where there is a narrow pass (Yazoo Pass), on the average between 60–100 feet wide but very deep and a lot of bother. By terrible patience and after laborious efforts, we were able to advance about 4–5 miles in a day from morning to evening.

On the 5th day, we had the 20-mile long pass behind us and into the Coldwater. The pass had been pretty well blocked on the lower end by guerrillas, you see, by felling large trees, which are numerous there and are well suited to a blockade. In many places, they are so close that their branches are friendly with one another

---

24 Diary, Apr. 9, 12, 13, 1863.

and can shake hands, and by chopping them down they intertwine and bathe their heads in the pass. It caused our men (regimenters from Helena under Genr. [Willis A.] Gorman) a lot of work and sweat to cut up the various colossuses and to fashion our way out of the pass again bit by bit, but after a week they had cleared the 20 miles.

On the banks of the pass there are only a few plantations bordering, since the ground is mostly swampy because of its depth, or it's under water. However, a large plantation is on the right bank of the pass, consisting of more than 100 acres, which was cultivated and in pretty good order while the others were mostly deserted. In general, the farms, formerly superabundant with cotton and other products, have suffered enormously since the war and are at most only half cultivated. The whites are completely gone and the Negro work (if there are Negroes there) is very little and independent, à la plaisire. Besides this bad situation it is also to be mentioned that all the levees on the Mississippi, as well as on the tributaries, are neglected and broken through in several places or even ripped out completely for miles, so that the waters of the mighty stream stretch for a large part, indeed the greater part of the shore and render cultivation of the fields impossible.

Now that we had the pass behind us and the Coldwater ahead of us, we entered into the snaky windings of the latter. The trip went much more quickly because, first, the boats were all already free of the decorations and woodwork, were thus trimmed for the fight, and second, the curves in the river were not so short and so close together as a pass and the river itself was a few paces wider. The smokestacks, which were very visible in battle and the continuous battling with the branches, were taken down. However, we on the *Romeo* didn't do it until the smokestack on the port side had found itself in a stubborn struggle with a mighty branch, and consequently had been stretched out lengthwise on the hurricane roof with a terrible noise. Well, it didn't cause any damage, just startled us a little for we believed that the ship was in the process of coming apart, and it saved us the trouble of taking it down.

The area around Coldwater began gradually to look a little more like civilization. The banks began to come to the forefront more frequently, plantations began to become more fruitful and many bore signs of great care and industry, having been used before the war to produce as many commodities as possible, and which still gave a fine and magnificent picture overall. But this is all altered now, for 2 years of neglect give a field a very run-down appearance and brings about great privation. It is just lucky that the loss falls hardest on those who are to blame for all the trouble.

I am also convinced that we can do much more damage to the South, and thereby bring it to the realization that they were asses and fools to attempt to ruin our country, if our army at the present would concentrate mainly on destroying the Southern plantations and means of production as much as possible rather than on pressuring them with powder and lead. Hunger is more powerful than powder and lead, and according to all appearances they would rather stay healthy than see themselves starve. From the last harvest they can't have much of a stockpile anymore, and they were hardly able to get this year's seed in the ground on account of all the rain. And spring here is going to be very late this year, by a whole month now, as a farmer here told me. I replied that I wished the South had seen that happen a year ago already.

We finally covered the 40 miles of the Coldwater to where it flows into the Tallahatchie on the 10th of March, without having any further adventures. The guerrillas that had been seen so much before did not appear at all.

This river is a little wider and more navigable than the above, but the journey was crippled here yet from significant curves and zigzags and it went only slightly better when we were in the Tallahatchie. But when we had some 40 miles behind us, it began to go significantly faster. And after putting the last 75 of the approximately 200 of the Tallahatchie behind us on the 12th, we docked at the place where someone took the liberty of yelling a booming "Halt!" to us and demanded to see our pass, which then was to be shown on the following day.

The area that we traversed on the last day on the Tallahatchie showed considerable improvement, and showed as a change from the previously flat and low, marshy area a little hill here and there that really looked more artificial than natural. Many suspected, as I also had to , that they were Indian graves, for they had mostly the same form and were symmetrical and went pretty sharply up in the air like a molehill in the flat area, about 40–50 or even 80–100 feet, just as wide and somewhat longer. I saw that the plantation owners often made use of these humps to put their houses on, thereby protecting them from the floods, or to put gardens in on them. And they used them in many ways, so that it drove you crazy wondering whether the Indians or the Southern knights had dug them up, unless you had also seen the hills just like these in the woods here and there where there was no plantation at all.

We are all hale and hearty, for the sun is shining again. Many greetings to all and all.

Your true Henry

The expedition had been halted after traveling only half its appointed distance. Kircher was back where he had started three months before and Vicksburg still stood defiantly on its high, strategic bluffs.

CHAPTER FIVE

"Joy and Unrest"

As spring settled in the Mississippi Valley, Grant's Vicksburg campaign entered its climactic phase. Grant planned to move down the Louisiana side and cross to the high ground south of town. Osterhaus's 9th division of McClernand's 13th Corps helped open a route through the low bottomland while the 12th Missouri, as part of Sherman's 15th Corps, waited at Young's Point. Kircher was allowed a few days of rest. The much-discussed policy of arming freed Negroes neared reality, and Kircher's correspondence revealed his qualified acceptance of that inevitable outgrowth of the war.

Ballard's Plantation, Young's Point
April 19th 1863

Dear Father!

I received your long and friendly letter of March 29th the day before yesterday. I can't call back into my memory everything that I wrote you a few months ago; the letter was probably pretty well garnished with fire, sword and hemp. If I expressed myself a little strongly you will no doubt forgive me for it, and in a year you will concede that I am right. For there won't be any peace in the land until it goes that far.

A people develops gradually. When it finally has grown to rebellion, only a miracle can tear it from its anger and put it back into balance again; then a terrible storm that, racing, tears away everything in its path and consumes whatever resists it. Therefore, I say that as long as there is still time it is preferable to direct and to soften it with a few examples in the form of a copperhead on the gallows. Why not do it? It will save the lives of many others who are far more deserving. Time will teach us whether such a mild head will accomplish this with a nation like this, more than a strict one at a time and in a country like this. It is said; "Whoever never gets angry, is also never good." A little burst of temper at the right time and place clears the air and you can breathe free again.

You mustn't get me wrong when I say I wouldn't like to fight with a black. By that I am only saying that I wouldn't like to be a slave boss, a slave driver, and fight at his side, mix my blood with his, perhaps be wounded by the same bullet that first traffics with a Negro and then pays me a visit. I am not far enough advanced in civilization that I don't know the difference between white and black anymore.

But still, despite all that, I don't have anything against it. On the contrary, I am quite satisfied, very much for it. Mother will perhaps remember that I spoke out for it already 1½ years ago, if it is carried out as proposed, that the black regiments don't come into any contact with the white ones. For as soon as this occurs our army will feel slighted, and gradually the difference between white and black will show less and less until it has disappeared. What is a white who forgets that he stands above the African? Then he is no better. The Negro would gain, if possible, in education, impudence and pride (that is, vanity: to dress up and shine like a brass monkey) as soon as he pays more attention to instruction. The latter two characteristics are naturally predominant. Because they were roughly treated much earlier one should think they would be thankful for a friendly word or deed; but on the contrary, then they believe they have the right to demand more and more. If you then complain they get rude. However, give them a kick and they comprehend very fast, become polite and say: dad da is a gentlem.

It may come from the education of the Southern gentlemen that they are that way, but that remains Gottlieb Schulze to me [irrelevant], and they will probably be that way as long as they exist.

In the regiment, there are some candidates for officers in the Negro regiments. I believe that the Negroes make tolerable soldiers. They possess all the necessary attributes, such as vanity, much greed and imagination. Their courage is not up to much, but not every soldier is courageous by a longshot, he just is when he has to be. Now we will hope for the best and the most successful.

A few days ago, there was somewhat of a cannonade here at the tongue of land vis-à-vis Vicksburg during the night, from the approximately 50 cannons of the fortress near Vicksburg and the gunboat *La Fayette* and a casemate battery that was composed of four 32-pd Parrots. It lasted about 1½ hours, until of our 8 ironclads and 3 transports all of the first got through, but one of the transports (*Henry Clay*) was set on fire by the enemy and sank after it had been burned down to the water level. This whole experiment cost us only 2 wounded on the ironclad *Benton* and the transport ship. That is quite successful if, out of 11 ships, only one is lost when they are peppered at that way.[1] Just imagine if about 50 large guns are spitting fire and iron what a tremendous spectacle that must be in a very dark night, and then the poisonous hissing and whining of the bullets and pieces of the same. Just believe me that if one has heard them once, one needs no convincing that they are making an attempt on one's life; one believes it without any proof. I wonder if an attack on Vicksburg will be made soon?

May the heartiest and most sincere greetings from me find you all healthy and well.

Your loyal son Henry

Camp Ballard's Plantation
Young's Point April 22nd 1863

Dear Mother!

Yesterday, something unusual for the army happened. Adjutant General [Lorenzo] Thomas was here and gave a short speech yesterday morning to Blair's division as well as the 17th and 12th Missouri volunteer regiments, who were also invited, since the rest of our division is at Greenville [Mississippi]. After we had formed a square of 10 men deep on a side a cannon shot was set off, the general sign to shut up. Then came Adjutant General Thomas, accompanied by General Sherman, Blair and their staffs, riding at full gallop, dismounted, and made their appearance in the middle of the square on a stage made of two wagons and some boards. We weren't allowed to get near enough to see A. G. Thomas's face for everybody had to remain in rank and file, even if he could neither hear nor see; which affected me so because I was, not to my good fortune, not such a tall fellow that I could see over all the heads. But I did get to hear something here and there and I could imagine the rest, which is just as good. I was only able to see that A. G. Thomas had an almost weak head and a tall, slim body that had bowed forward a little and that the whole figure was dressed in a U.S. uniform.

In his speech, or better his assignment, he was to inform the soldiers that the cabinet and the president had decided that the most effective way to weaken the South would be to take up the

---

[1] The action occurred on the night of Apr. 16, when seven gunboats and three transports ran the Vicksburg gauntlet to cooperate with Grant's infantry downriver. The *Henry Clay* was burned and the *Benton* lost one killed and three wounded. *OR*, vol. 24, pt. 1, 517.

Negro slaves in our army as quickly as possible and use them as purposefully as possible, be it as soldiers, laborers or whatever, in order to spare the soldiers as much as possible.

But since they could not be used any more advantageously than if they were regularly organized into regiments with white officers leading them, he was here at hand to organize two regiments of these Free Americans of African Descent.

However, the soldiers are not to think that these regiments of Free A's. of A.D. are to be equal to the white regiments, in no way, for they are a subordinate race and would be used chiefly for such labors as previously fell as a burden to the white soldiers. And they will be used as soldiers chiefly to fight against guerrillas, as they know the area, the terrain, etc., better and therefore could often beat back the enemy more quickly and more powerfully.

All those who felt that they were diligent enough, whether they be privates or officers, should report to their division's commander and would be immediately commissioned as colonels or other officers after being recommended to him (Adjt. G. Tho.) by a Board of Officers set up for that purpose, and would be immediately placed in a position in one of the Negro regiments suitable to their rank. But he wanted only those men of whom he is convinced that they are dedicated with their entire souls to their duty as such. He was also empowered to remove any officer under his command on the spot, no matter who he might be, who worked against this above mentioned matter by his speech or his actions.

Such was the approximate content of Adjutant General Thomas's speech or narrative. At least that's what it seemed more like to me. It seemed just as if he or the government didn't have the courage simply to command and to require obedience. By God, the soldiers have sworn to be loyal to the government and will be loyal, with few exceptions. If not, and they do what is described in the Articles of War as is required, he should be placed before a war tribunal, and according to its verdict be shot without further ado, as befits a traitor, a dog. If that would happen once or twice then there would be no more black sheep among the whites, for those few would soon be gray, and then they would be as good as the white sheep.

General Sherman was then called up and made a short speech that contained pretty much the same or at least supported it, and concluded by saying: "Everybody has his opinion, I have mine, General Blair has his and we all have ours, although they may not be the same on this subject, but we are soldiers and have sworn to be true to our cause, which is a just one, and support we must our Government and we will, and we shall obey it in every respect." General Blair followed then said no more. Then 2 colonels, whom I didn't know, and in conclusion Col. Hassendeubel, who said the same thing in German.

Thereupon A. G. Thomas proposed 3 hurrahs for the President, which were gladly and joyfully thundered into the sky, then 3 more for the policy of our government, which had the same result, although a little stronger. Then General Sherman proposed 3 for A. G. Thomas, which followed immediately, and since everybody was already hurrahing, several suggested 3 for Sherman, Blair, etc.; but they got weaker and weaker. Well, the speakers were to blame for that; they couldn't keep the men entertained during their campaign speeches and they encouraged roaring more than keeping quiet, perhaps? But here everything seemed forced, as if it was done only from a sense of duty and not from conviction. Much better would be not to say anything to the soldiers, such as how they like this or that. They are long since accustomed to obedience, to the "must," and prefer that to a timidity that is just laughable.

After the last dwindling hurrahs, the Star Spangled Banner was played and then the cannon that had long been eagerly awaited by most of the men boomed out from its thundering mouth; the signal to dismiss roared and we promptly obeyed it, and made ourselves comfortable at our meal and had the afternoon [to ourselves]. The clouds, which had been pacing back and forth in the sky all day long with a dark face, were relieved of their melancholy as a breeze cleansed the air and made it less humid; just a quiet time to gather one's thoughts.

Thus went yesterday, and in the evening there were already several applications for a Negro commission made to the Colonel.

[April] 23rd. The talk around camp is that General Osterhaus and his division have crossed the Mississippi below Vicksburg at the railroad by Carthage and taken 500 prisoners there.[2] I can't decide what is true about that and what is not. Unfortunately, I don't believe that General Osterhaus will succeed in getting us back under his command, despite his attempts.

The friendliest and heartiest greetings to you all from

your loyal son Henry

---

[2] Osterhaus had not yet crossed the river and the rumor of 500 prisoners was untrue.

Camp Ballard's Plantation
Near Vicksburg April 25th 1863

Dear Mother!

In haste, I want to inform you that we just received marching orders that tell us to be "ready to march at a minute's notice" tomorrow or the next day, to land on steamboats as far as Milliken's Bend, 12–15 miles above. Then with as little baggage as possible, 10 days rations, on the train to Richmond, and then to march from there to Carthage on the Mississippi. Then on the 8 transports that luckily got past the blockade on the River of all Rivers, and in this way to get in back of Vicksburg; time will tell what we do there. There are no bluffs there and it is consequently not so strongly fortified. Besides, we will destroy the railroad link with Jackson, the bridge on the Big Black. When this is accomplished, then there is only the narrow land pass between the Yazoo and the Big Black, which is not sufficient to supply a large army with provisions. They will have to evacuate Vicksburg. We all have a lot of faith in this expedition, and everybody is revived with the thought that finally something is being done.[3]

I would estimate our forces at 30,000–40,000, 2 of Farragut's cannon boats (each with 20–25 cannons), additionally 8 ironclads from Admiral Porter's fleet.[4] Ten ironclads are capable of sweeping a stretch of 10 miles of shore and 2–3 miles inland, which would be an area of 20–30 square miles. If they can make this stretch unsafe for the enemy, then we will be safe.

Thousands of the heartiest and friendliest greetings from me to all, large and small.

Your loyal Henry

All the troops except the 12th and 17th Missouri left Young's Point on April 26. The departure of his regiment was delayed one day and Kircher noted that the change of scenery came just in time. As the Mississippi fell, it exposed muddy banks that had been flooded for weeks. The soggy vegetation began to rot in the warm spring sunshine, a condition the young lieutenant considered unhealthy. He reached Milliken's Bend with his regiment on the twenty-eighth. Beer and other liquors waited there to cheer the troops as they prepared for the grand envelopment of Vicksburg. "Consequence is

---

[3] Kircher's strategic sense was admirable and his comments indicate that at least a few of Grant's lower echelon officers were well posted on the campaign's developments.

[4] Farragut commanded the naval forces cooperating with Banks's campaign against Port Hudson. He ran some of his vessels past the Rebel guns there in an effort to control the Mississippi between it and Vicksburg.

that sprees are in fashion and the Guard house is well crowded with the Lions (beasts) of the day."[5]

The 12th Missouri moved out on May 2 for Hard Times Landing, fifteen miles south of Vicksburg, where Grant's army prepared to cross the river. The roads were rugged and the weather humid. Kircher complained of Steele's marching orders: "he rather is a fool or tri[e]s to kill us, marching allwas in the greatest heat of day. And at that draging along, stopping, and a rush is of what our marches consists." Despite that, Kircher reached Hard Times on May 6. After resting a few hours, the soldiers boarded boats to cross the wide river. They were on Vicksburg's side by midnight.[6]

For Kircher, the campaign quickly developed into several days of rigorous marching that kept him and his men very close to the fighting but never in it. The army followed the course he far-sightedly outlined in an earlier letter, with Steele's division leaving the river on May 8. Kircher did not follow. He was detached to command a guard placed over commissary stores. It gave him a chance to visit an acquaintance in the commissary department and to feast on "luxurious and delicate" fare, but he longed to rejoin his regiment. Sent as guard for a wagon train dispatched to feed the advancing soldiers, he did just that on May 11.[7]

Marching in the wake of Grant's fast-moving army, Kircher observed that few civilians remained in their homes. Like the storekeeper in Cayuga who posted a sign, "Clossed up untill the war is over," they had left for safer places. Kircher came close to finding battle on May 12 when units of his brigade skirmished with Rebel cavalry. He did not participate, but pressed a flower from the field between his diary pages, where it remains today. One wounded Rebel was found when the enemy fled. He was taken to the hospital, where an injured 17th Missouri man recognized him as his brother. "Who can tell if they have not shot at [each other], such is civil war."[8]

When Kircher reached Jackson on May 14, he found its entrenchments empty, the town deserted. Soldiers and officers helped themselves to what they could find. Kircher thought the scene was disgusting; "it should be carried on in a deacent way, and not any one allowed to destroy as suits his notion. We are not robers."[9]

The campaign's momentum continued. While the other units of Grant's army fought two sharp and decisive battles, Kircher trudged behind with his regiment. On May 18, he saw the rear of Vicksburg for the first time. Skirmishing cost the 12th Missouri some casualties that day. More men were lost on the nineteenth when the army consolidated its cordon around Vicksburg. Kircher and his men skirmished all day, driving to the

[5] Diary, Apr. 26, 27, 30, 1863.
[6] Diary, May 2, 4, 6, 1863.
[7] Diary, May 8–11, 1863.
[8] Diary, May 11, 12, 1863.
[9] Diary, May 15, 1863.

Mississippi's old river bed north of town. The terrible bluffs that had blocked Sherman the Christmas before were taken and supply boats unloaded necessary material.[10]

A siege was in the making, but Grant tried to crack Vicksburg's defenses before committing his men to such a time-consuming operation. On May 22, he ordered assaults all along the line. At some points they made headway, catching a foothold here and there on the rugged Rebel fortifications, but none promised a breakthrough. From McClernand, whose corps stood southeast of Vicksburg, came word that his troops were on the verge of cutting through. He erroneously believed his men's limited penetrations were important. Grant, who was on another part of the line, did not trust his subordinate's judgment but wanted to avoid the consequences of misreading McClernand's progress. He ordered further assaults by the other two corps of his army.

Earlier that day, the 12th Missouri had marched about a mile and a half toward the army's left, crossing three spaces open to enemy fire, and by late afternoon stood waiting at its assigned staging area. When Grant's order filtered down the chain of command, the regiment went forward. It proved to be the 12th Missouri's bloodiest afternoon, a miscalculation that needlessly threw one of Sherman's best units against solid enemy works. The assault failed and resulted in many casualties.[11]

Camp [north] of Vicksburg May 24th 1863

Dear Mother!

I am only now getting a chance to write a few lines. Oh, if I hadn't lived through the past 3 days.

That we have taken Jackson and left it after everything that the enemy can use was destroyed you will surely know from the newspapers. At noon on the 18th, we arrived here before the fortifications of Vicksburg, which begin at a distance of approximately 4 miles from the Court House all around and which supposedly go into the town proper. The area all around is Switzerland, as many who could know call it, and almost every hill is crowned with a fort and with a collar of rifle pits. These must now all be taken from the enemy or they must be starved out in order to take the city. We have them completely surrounded, Sherman (our Army Corps) on the river above Vicksburg, [James B. McPherson's 17th] Army Corps in the center and [McClernand's] on the left below Vicksburg.

Now, until a few days ago everything was going pretty well.

---

[10] Diary, May 18–20, 1863.
[11] Bruce Catton, *Grant Moves South* (Boston, 1960), 452–53.

We had driven them to the heights 2 miles from the city but they had a smaller area to defend, and every morning we can see new forts, rifle pits and earthworks.

They seem to be waiting for significant help from Bragg,[12] otherwise they wouldn't be so stubborn, with 29–30,000 men fighting against 60,000 that have them in a closed position. Now from the 22d on was the most terrible, cruelest time so far for us (the 12th regiment) that we have experienced.

If you use quite a bit of imagination, you can perhaps get an idea of the road, or better the little pathway that we had to follow. We reached the point of assembly by marching and climbing from 10 A.M. to 12 noon. We were beset by heavy musket fire at the first [open] place for about 50 yards, the second about 30 yards, and the third and the worst one 75 strides.

It was always one company after the other, so that there was no crowding. The 25th Iowa was the first, the 12th Missouri, the 3d Missouri, 17th Missouri and 26th Iowa.

My company (K), the color guard, was the 5th [company] of the 12th [Missouri]. When the entire company went through double quick, Friedrich, who should have been farther forward, didn't want to go on, and I drew my saber half out of its sheath and asked "Forward or not?" After a little hesitation he got going nice and proper. Here we all (Company K) were able to get through safely. But Captain [Christian] Andel, whose loss I feel deeply, fell here, hit by a piece of shell, dead, as if struck by lightning. It went into his right shoulder and came out between the last rib and the hip. It must have taken heart, liver, lung and almost everything. He had no pain, a death of misfortune.

Then it went on to the last blockade. My captain was hit through the left hip (a flesh wound). Finally at 5 P.M., we were all (who hadn't fallen) positioned down below on the hill. The command "Forward" was given in a lively voice by Gen. Steele, Gen. [John M.] Thayer and Col. [Charles R.] Woods (commander of our brigade). The 9th Iowa (good, brave, undaunted soldiers) came first, then the 12th and the rest.

It was about 200 yards to a point in front of the rifle pits that were full of sharpshooters, who sent a murderous hail of bullets into our ranks. Through the latter we now had to climb the steep

---

12 Braxton Bragg commanded the Army of Tennessee in central Tennessee.

hills as fast as possible, over tree trunks and brush. How those who survived survived God knows, I can't comprehend it.

But it kept going forward, the 9th in the lead and the 12th hot on their heels; the other regiments more or less left us completely in the lurch. They just shot one of us here and there in the back, the wretched ones. We lay still 10–15 paces in front of the enemy fortifications, as we saw that nobody was following, and we had too few remaining to make a further attempt until it was dark. We then began to climb back down, taking our wounded with us, as many as we could.[13] But I can't describe all this, for I didn't get done with all the wounded until today an hour ago, taking them to the hospital. They must all be taken over the hill with stretchers and then carried for a mile. The first could only occur at night, as during the day the rebels shot at us as soon as we gave them a glimpse of us.

Of the regiment, 15 officers are now dead or wounded and 113 men in the same fix. A third of the entire 12th regiment murdered, only because Sherman thinks that everything can be forced by the stormers without knowing the terrain or testing it out. Capt. Andel dead, Lieut. [Casimir] Andel lies wounded in the right arm, Capt. Affleck wounded in the leg and others that you don't know.[14]

But I see that we can't send any letters from here at all, only by opportunity. G. Grant has forbidden us to send letters, but we can receive them. An order came today from Grant that the enemy is so strong that, on the contrary, no more stormers may be used.

Your loyal son

In a diary entry dated May 22 but written several days later, Kircher poured out his bitterness. "It was a sade scene to see so many brave boys slaughtered without having accomplished any thing. It very *foolish* of our Commanders to take all these troops by three blockades during daylight [;] in doing so he of course notified the enemy of our coming and showed the strength of our attacking party so it could not be any surprize for the enemy which if it had been we would have carried the works.

---

[13] Woods reported that the 12th Missouri was "repulsed before the other regiments of the brigade could reach the top of the hill. The four right companies, having more favorable ground to move upon, reached a covered position near the foot of the enemy's breastworks, and were obliged to remain until dark before they could be recalled." *OR*, vol. 24, pt. 2, 252.
[14] The regiment's service records listed a total loss of 112 men, 31.1 percent of those engaged. Hess, "The 12th Missouri Infantry: A Socio-Military Profile of a Union Regiment," *Missouri Historical Review* 76, no. 1 (1981): 66.

"But strategy mi boy! Why did not the great charger S[herman] come and lead it himself, show or at least tell us which road to take[;] but no, only orders are given to charge up the hill and take the pits. had we been sent up during some night and advanced on the enemy before he new it we could have succeed[ed] . . . those that advanced were brave, or else they would not go through such an auful hail of bullets . . .

"It made the tears come to my eyes, as I was urging my brave company forward and seeing them drop one after the other like flies from the first frost. Oh! may I never witness such a sight again. But as soldiers we had and were, and are willing to obey orders from our superior officers. But may this be the last fit of insanity that our commanders will ever have."

Camp near Vicksburg May 26th 1863

Dear Mother!

You must really have more patience than I think you have if you aren't angry about my few letters in the recent time. But if you could have seen us when we arrived in camp in the evening after our latest marches, how happy we were to spread out our wounded limbs on the then soft ground and how we sank into a deep sleep, even sometimes rather missing the evening meal, then you would understand. Besides that, we were not allowed to bring blankets along. Only two wagons went per regiment. I took a few printed envelopes with paper, also ink, but forgot my pen. Besides, no letters go out from here unless one can smuggle them out, although the mail arrives properly. Now just be patient, and when victory is ours everything will go well again. In the first place, it can't last much longer, for they are living, if one can say that, on donkey meat and ½ rations. Such a life will make even a secesh disgusted fast. Every day 3–6 deserters come to us and say the same thing, so it must be true.

Bert was slightly wounded, as Casimir was, and they get a leave. They already left yesterday by boat up the river. You will see them. They can tell you better than anybody can write. I just can't comprehend how I and so many others came back unscathed. Now I believe, by God, that no bullet is for me.

Bliesner arrived here today and brought my chest. My heartiest thanks for everything. They were quite suitable goodies for us, only everything would have tasted better to me if the recently and so shamefully dead and wounded friends had been in the group and the good things had all been shared. But what good is feeling troubled? We are soldiers and who the next bullet hits must accept it. The past can't be altered. Now comes an order from Grant that no more taking by storm shall be attempted. When the child falls in the well, then cover it!

By the way, all the generals were supposedly greatly opposed to this last storm, but Grant wouldn't let himself be stopped and still gave the order for the entire line to charge. As a reply, the rebels gave us such a terrible hail of bullets as neither I nor anybody had ever heard before; it was terrible! Besides, out of the 6 regiments, only the 9th Iowa and ours went forward properly, only individual companies of the others. The 3rd went fairly well and, I only know from Capt. [George] Schuster and his company [C], they got as close as 10–15 steps from the enemy rifle pits. The 17th (Col. Hassendeubel's, sick in Milliken's Bend) stayed way back and had only 2 or 3 or no wounded. Now, it was better that we didn't take them (the rifle pits), because I think I saw cannons hidden in them that showered it lengthwise, so that those who really did get in [would have been] buried in a ditch by Kartätschen.[15]

But I can tell you that there were tears in my eyes when I saw the brave 9th Iowa advancing and the 12th, with heap upon heap dead or wounded, making one last energetic thrust, sometimes into the bayonet of a friend, falling to the ground and still crying out in a firm and loud voice "Forward!" to his friends. That has to unnerve anybody, no matter how tough he might be. I must say that I only heard very few of the many lying around me utter any sounds or screams. They were soldiers! I as well as Bert and Joe, my best friend here, gave Lieutenant Andel my diary and a letter to take along.

Your loyal son

The blunted attacks convinced Grant that only a siege could pry the Rebels out of Vicksburg. The 12th Missouri began to make itself at home as Kircher recorded in his diary the work needed to clean up the aftermath of the futile assault. Rebel fire on attempts to remove the wounded angered Kircher. "Were I in command . . . the last man in Vicksburg would be shot as soon as we have them." Fresh earthworks appeared every morning in the enemy lines; "they must rute up the ground aufully." Shovels and hoes were issued for their own "ruting," as the Federals sank themselves into the Mississippi earth. The tools were also used for more sorrowful purposes. Kircher noted meticulously the exact spot where he helped bury Christian

---

[15] Canister, case, grapeshot, or shrapnel.

Andel. Four days after the fight, a two-and-a-half-hour truce allowed the Federals to recover and bury the rest of their dead. The tragedy of May 22 eased Kircher's interstate prejudice; the fallen Missourians, he noted, were "just as brave" as the Illinoisans.[16]

In their camp north of Vicksburg, the regimenters received their baggage, shipped from Milliken's Bend, and could change clothes for the first time in a month. When they looked at the flag supplied by the Belleville ladies, they discovered more than half a dozen holes in the fabric and the staff shot in two; it would have been further riddled had not the bearer fallen early in the attack.[17]

Settled in for a long wait, Kircher took time to prepare a summary of the campaign for his father.

Camp Walnut Hills at Vicksburg Miss
May 30th 1863

Dear Father!

When we got to Grand Gulf, our troops had already taken it and both Army Corps (McClernand's and McPherson's) had marched off to Jackson. The area on the other side of the river that we had behind us in three days, as you will see in my diary, consists of flat, everywhere swampy land, but still very productive, one large and magnificent plantation after the other. Really, one can't imagine what else the Southern knights wanted. They had regular palaces (*had* because our soldiers have burned them down, for the most part, whether on order or not I don't know), and thousands of acres with complete villages of nothing but houses for Negroes and complete workshops too, gardens; everything, everything that a person could possibly wish for to make life pleasant. But they had too much. They didn't want to be princes any more, no, emperors and czars. the whites wanted [the Negroes] under the whip. Now, one after the other will lose house and home; yes, almost shirt and trousers, everything, even their lives. It also costs many a better, nobler life lost. But it is the just punishment. The last one must go to the scaffold and then it will be peaceful. But I am getting carried away.

The gunboats, as usual, claim to have taken Port Gibson and Grand Gulf. To be sure, they reported to Grant that the ports had been silenced. But when the transports and troops went past to land on this shore, the rebel batteries again began murderous fire

---

[16] Diary, May 23, 24, 26, 1863.
[17] Diary, May 28, 1863.

and had simply kept silent out of treachery, as they had noticed that the transports wanted to get through.

Well, despite everything, everything went well and the boats escaped with a few holes. Our troops attacked the enemy at Port Gibson, about 12,000 men strong, as soon as they had gotten a firm foothold, drove them to flight, took 500–600 captives and marched behind Grand Gulf then to take the fort; but the rebels had already left it.[18] Now the gun silencers land, take a paintbrush and paint with them right away and write on the three spiked cannons, "captured by Rear Admiral Porter's gunboats." And the troops had actually taken them, at least defeated the enemy, which is the main thing.

Arriving in Grand Gulf, I had to stay behind with 30 men to guard commissary stores. But since I don't like to be gone from my regiment, namely when a battle is coming up, I plagued the commissar long enough that he finally gave me permission after 3 days to push back to my regiment, which I did on the morning of the following day. At noon of the same day, the 3d and 17th Missouri of our brigade had a little skirmishing. We were also ordered out, but it was just a couple hundred enemy cavalry who, after they saw us press forward en masse, gave their horses the spurs, and we also got to see that.

On the following day, we came through Raymond over the battlefield of McPherson and Johnston.[19] There were a great number of butternut-colored logs and scraps lying all around. It had rained toward evening; consequently, we spent that night by a constant fire in order to get dry. The next morning, we still had 14–15 miles to march yet to Jackson. We started out at 7 or 7:30 and around 9:00 it began to rain quite splendidly, and it rained all day, sometimes drenching, sometimes less, so that marching in the loamy soil was very difficult and tiring for us. But towards 4 o'-clock, we arrived before Jackson and received the order to stay there in battle lines as we were supposed to advance right away.

Soon there came the order to proceed. We went through a young forest off to the right from the main road, appropriated the railroad that leads to Vicksburg and wanted to attack the rifle pits

---

[18] Kircher accurately traced the course of events but his estimates of Confederate strength and losses were exaggerated. The Rebels had more than 5,000 men at Port Gibson and lost 384 taken prisoner. *OR*, vol. 24, pt. 1, 667.

[19] Brig. Gen. John Gregg of Joseph E. Johnston's command, not Johnston himself, led the Rebels at Raymond.

there right away, just as we heard that they had already been deserted and that Jackson was ours. We now marched with a waving banner with an enormous roar of jubilation, and moved on to the west side of the city to camp; or, more accurately, we bivouacked.

Then all the soldiers stormed into Jackson, as they heard that there was no provost guard in the city, and began to plunder all the stores, just plain looting them. Whatever they couldn't eat or use was trampled into the mud, as I heard. I only saw one street of the city, for the next day we had to start destroying the railroad and were only able to take a small part in the celebrations. Also, on Grant's orders, all public houses and whatever could possibly be useful to the rebels was destroyed by fire. Later I heard that some of our couriers remained behind when we marched out and were murdered. For this, the State House and Court House were supposed to have been almost completely burned down as well; there were only a few heaps of ashes left to bear witness to the capital of Mississippi. It seems that the rebels didn't think Jackson was in danger until just shortly before the capture. It wasn't fortified; we just saw communications trenches, but even these were thrown up in a hurry.

Our invasion was quite a daring venture, but there was much to be gained if it succeeded, which it has indeed done thus far. As long as we were on the march the rebels didn't know where we would strike next, for all roads in all directions were filled with our troops. One army corps would lay hold of the enemy and defeat him, or the corps would move back until another corps would join with it and they both advanced. And the enemy, soon overwhelmed, would have to run away with heavy losses or give themselves up. This is how we advanced in the 16 days before Jackson, and on the 17th [day] we had already enveloped Vicksburg.

To be sure, we have been around Vicksburg since the 18th of this month and have probably wedged in the enemy significantly, but nothing is going to change. We must use patience and a little hunger advantage. As all of the deserters, of whom there are very many, say, they will soon be played out. A small piece of cornbread and a very small piece of bacon is all they live on.

Very probably, they will make an attempt to break through our line by storm, and that could bring them to an end with great losses. But then they would still not be across the Big Black, which would be very difficult for them, for everywhere they would run into our troops and be properly surrounded. Our whole army can trample on their backs, so that they will have to finally surrender or all of the enemy will have to be killed. If an army of 30–40,000 rebels doesn't attack us from the rear, Vicksburg can't be helped, and where would the rebels want to take away such a force without weakening that point too much?

Many, many hearty greetings to everybody and everyone.

Your obedient son Henry

As May flowed into June and the Mississippi sun grew warmer, the siege developed a rhythm of ditching, sniping at Rebel targets, and efforts to kill time. Deserters regularly entered Federal lines bringing stories of empty dinner plates. One Rebel could not believe his enemies received meat and a loaf of bread "he thought big enough to feed half the Garrison of Vicksb." Locked in close proximity, men of opposing sides fraternized. "Some very interesting chat is Kapt up for a part of the evening most every night, between our and the rebel Pickets. This may be quite interesting for the parties engaged, but still ought not to be allowed."[20]

With the army stationary indefinitely, an opportunity for visits from hometown friends was presented. Henry Goedeking and "the fat" Dr. Ferdinand Rubach arrived on June 3, bringing three half barrels of beer as a gift. Kircher was quite pleased to see his "uncle" and escorted him in a walk along the breastworks, examining the Rebel lines with a field glass. They rode to the Big Black River, where Osterhaus commanded troops guarding Grant's rear.[21] During the course of his visit, Goedeking began to think like a soldier. "Uncle likes it here quite well and says he doesn't feel quite right unless cannons are thundering all about him and there is a ball flying over him."[22]

On June 8, Kircher accompanied his visitors to the landing to secure passage home. The *City of Alton*, chartered by Governor Yates to transport wounded soldiers north, offered berths to civilians. Kircher was amused by the attention doctors and female nurses gave a wounded soldier on the boat. "Every one had either a fan, and was fanning the poor man with such vivacity, that had he not been a tolerable fat man, would have been blowen off, or a cup with tea, water, coffee or the devil Knows what all [.] and the different doctors were discoirsing wether the poor defender of his country ought to have his leg or Head or arm (he was slightly wounded in the thigh) amputated, or have some Castor oil or some other dam stuff." For an unexplained reason, Goedeking and Rubach lost their berths aboard the *City of Alton* and steamed northward on the *Diligent*.[23]

The siege's regularity continued. Kircher and his men helped build an

[20] Diary, June 1, 2, 1863.
[21] Diary, June 3–5, 1863.
[22] Henry Kircher to "All!," June 7, 1863.
[23] Diary, June 8, 10, 1863.

earthwork, named Fort Lightfoot to honor the 12th Missouri's major who had been killed on the twenty-second. Rain descended on June 10 to create muddy mounds of the new breastworks that stretched across the hills and through a peach orchard near the 12th Missouri's camp. The downpour washed soldiers out of their tents and sleeping holes, forcing them to repair the works. Kircher amused himself now and then by taking potshots at anything that moved in the Rebel lines. One day, a Confederate picket told his Union counterpart that the Rebels had a new commander-in-chief, "General Starvation." "A rather stubborn old Companion," Kircher thought.[24]

The previous campaign and the assault of May 22 were still very much on the young lieutenant's mind.

Camp Walnut Hills Miss June 17th 1863

Dear Mother!

"Who was the poor soldier that almost starved on the way to Jackson and here?" Hardly one of my friends, or maybe he wrote such nonsense as that just to have something to write or something to brag about to his relatives. I say that nobody can reproach General Grant, whether he is responsible for it or not, at all about the entire campaign since Milliken's Bend on May 2d until the 22d. Imagine an army of 60–70 thousand men marching about 150 miles, that had to cross the Mississippi once with only 7 steamboats at its disposal, that defeats the enemy under way 4 times, so that he loses his shoes as well as 84 cannons and 5,000 prisoners; the capital of the State of Mississippi with all its glass factories, spinning mills and the like; the rail connections between Mobile, Richmond, Vicksburg and New Orleans (naturally also the cities in between as well) and torn up around Jackson for 5 miles in every direction. And then finally to top it all off, after these 20 days, 20–30,000 men sitting on the fortifications of Vicksburg.

And one day we didn't have any coffee and one day everyone had just one cracker, while the usual ration was about 3½. On the other hand there were cattle, the finest oxen, in abundance all along the way just waiting for slaughter. On every plantation there were large vegetable gardens with good stands, etc. Anybody who wasn't lazy didn't need to suffer from hunger.

In Jackson, all of Sherman's corps masqueraded and got drunk and played the fool. Now what else does a soldier want? I admit that we have had to undergo hardships, but the soldier who sees

---

[24] Diary, June 9, 10, 11, 16, 1863.

that something has a purpose and who doesn't want to endure any hardships would not be worth my lifting up my foot to give him a kick in the behind, unless it would be possibly to see just for fun how a lazybones absorbs his just deserts.

Father is quite right to get angry at such a scoundrel as would take pleasure at the Bellevillers who fell here. But my plan would not be to shoot him, no; I would give $15 to a Negro and he would beat him black and blue for 24 hours until all desire to take pleasure in that would vanish.

Mr. [Frederick] Rupp could do me the favor in his newspaper [the *Belleviller Zeitung*] of correcting quite especially the following. 1.) That Col. Wangelin was absent during the charge on the 22nd is a lie, no matter who makes that claim. He has his short-comings, perhaps too many to make a good colonel, but he doesn't know cowardice. He was still with the regiment when it was under fire, always at his place if not, as was frequently the case, too far forward to call it reasonable, let alone cowardly.

Anyway, this comes from ex-Lt. Schierenberg, who had a dispute with the colonel because the former is supposed to have told him (Schierenberg) that he was a drunken fellow, in which the colonel was not very far from the truth either, or I don't know what else was the matter.[25] All I know is that Schierenberg has been stationed at the [St. Louis] *Westliche Post* as a loudmouth, complainer, crybaby, liar and I don't know what all else (the rest censored by the editor), and the colonel promised before he left that his name wouldn't appear in the paper if he could help it. Whatever they had between them, it is a pitiful way to get revenge on someone by bellowing out a lie about him into the world outside.

2.) That the 9th Iowa stood there and didn't go to the fore is again an infamous lie. The 9th Iowa was the first regiment in front; we were following hard on their heels, so let us both be cut down. But I have said I have spoken only the truth, that no regiment could have done a better job in the front than they. They lost, out of 250–270 men who went into the fight, 130 in the few minutes; in other words, more than 1/3 of their people in not more

---

[25] Lt. Ernst Schierenberg resigned in December, 1862, citing weak eyesight as his reason. Wangelin wholeheartedly endorsed the resignation, citing Schierenberg's inefficiency as an officer. Ernst Schierenberg to Hugo Wangelin, Nov. 25, 1862; Hugo Wangelin to H. Z. Curtis, Dec. 17, 1862, Ernst Schierenberg service record, NA.

than 5 minutes.[26] Why then did the 17th (Turner Rifles) not lose a single man, and still other regiments too? (There the dog is buried; there's the rub.)

The flag of the 9th Iowa color guard was straight in front of me, about 8–10 paces from the enemy. In order to secure the flag, for they thought like most that we would all be shot dead or taken prisoner, they passed it down from one to the other until it reached below safely.

Now, luckily for us, the rebels were too cowardly to come out of the communications trenches, or else they would even have been able to mow us down quickly too. I repeat that the 9th Iowa went foward well, and I could hardly hold back my tears as I saw how they and our regiment's bands had to fall back. And the [9th Iowa] was always in front, until finally our ranks were so thin and no more regiments came to our aid, and only then did we give up. We were no more than 10–15 paces from the enemy rifle pits. Naturally, some were farther back or perhaps some even closer. I couldn't see that well. But the regiments that were supposed to support us—where were they? Only the 3d Missouri moved forward, many as far as we did.[27]

I am sorry that I didn't take Uncle on the sunken *Cincinnati* when he was here.[28] I was there today. From there, one has a magnificent view of the whole defenses in the front and left wing of Vicksburg fortifications and of the city proper. Deserters keep coming still. Last night 4 came and said they have only bread made from rice flour, the pea bread is all gone.

In Vicksburg there must really be little food, for this evening I already heard many soldiers speculating about rats that ran over their faces, etc. If their rats are coming, the rebels must also be soon tamed.

Your Henry

June continued to unfold and the Rebels still hung on. They repaid

---

[26] The 9th Iowa, as officially reported, lost 78 men of less than 300 engaged, a ratio of approximately 26 percent. *OR*, vol. 24, pt. 2, 254.

[27] The 3d Missouri lost eighteen men that day but there is no official indication that it advanced as close to the Rebel works as did Kircher's regiment. Ibid., 162.

[28] The ironclad *Cincinnati* was sunk by Confederate fire on May 27. It settled in two to three feet of Mississippi River water on a sandbar, where it remained as a target for both Union salvage parties and Rebel artillery. Diary, May 27, 1863.

Federal fire in kind; several men of the 12th Missouri were hit from time to time and Kircher suffered at least two near misses. "While at dinner a rebel rifle ball was impudent enough to strike one of the tent poles about 2 feet above our heads . . . , it would be a rather rough joak to have beans mixed with blue ones. In the afternoon a rebel rifle ball passed through the top of our tent, big fuss but no one hurt."[29]

When not fending off Confederate missiles, Kircher helped with work on the siege lines, a project that seemed to have no end. Working parties removed the sunken *Cincinnati*'s guns at night when sharp-eyed Rebel artillerists had trouble drawing an accurate bead on them. Kircher went with one such expedition on the night of June 25, "rather exciting sport," he thought. Every ten minutes a Confederate ball came over, but lookouts yelled an alarm when they saw the guns flash so the party could jump into rifle pits dug for that purpose. "After hard labor and considerable of runing" they salvaged three pieces. The march back to camp proved to be a blind groping in pitch black night. Kircher kept himself in the road only "by stooping to the ground and feeling for the wagon track."[30]

By month's end, Confederate resistance visibly approached the breaking point. Deserters brought word of threatened mutiny in some units, as well as reports that the Rebel daily ration consisted of six ounces of bacon, one ounce of flour and five ounces of peas. By the beginning of July, Kircher noticed that an occasional shot into Vicksburg elicited no reply from its defenders. At 4:30 on the morning of July 4, the regiment formed ranks and stacked its arms. "It is very quiet [;] did my eyes not tell me different I would suppose I had been moved during the night, hearing not a Gun fired no wind stir [.] All in a profound silence." Kircher waited as the morning hours ticked quietly by until 10 o'clock. "What is it that all at once the air trembles with shouts, hurrah and gay faces meet all along on the breastworks. It tells us yes 'Vicksburg is ours.' "[31]

Camp Walnut Hills Miss July 4th 63

Dear Mother!

Yesterday noon, a group consisting of 3 officers bearing a flag of truce came to Grant to talk with 3 officers appointed by Grant to determine the conditions of the surrender of Vicksburg.

But Grant said; "It is no use, say 'Enough' and I will march into Vicksburg and you are my prisoners and you need not hurrah."

They had to withdraw with long faces, and said that in the last 24 hours they hadn't consumed more than 2 ounces of food.

---

[29] Diary, June 21, 1863.
[30] Diary, June 26, 1863.
[31] Diary, June 29, July 1, 4, 1863.

But Grant gave them time to consider until 10:00 today. Until then, neither side is supposed to shoot, but if Pemberton has not decided by then to surrender unconditionally (the poor fellow has nothing to eat and should give himself up, broken), we are prepared to give him a load of pills such as has never been sent before. We were all looking forward to the terrible cannonade of 200 cannons, or perhaps more when they all let go, and at least every 5 minutes each one can send a new ball. Five to six hours would go by with over 16,000 balls; but they all load much faster, about twice as fast. Add the mortars to that. That would have been a 4th of July celebration like no other. Our fort, Lightfoot, is also "ready for action," with a 40-pounder from the *Cincinnati*. It is commanded by J. Ledergerber and manned by our men.

And then the accursed fellows had to spoil our fun of shooting them. At 4:30 A.M. they raised the white flag. At 10 they began to draw up and they made "stack arms," and at 11 our troops marched in, I believe only McPherson's Corps. All in all, it is a joy and a double celebration, Vicksburg and the Fourth of July.

We have marching orders. That means to keep ourselves with 10 days provisions ready to march any minute. Some think we will go to help Banks, others to make hell hot for Johnston or Bragg! Of course, we would sweat more than a little in that kind of heat.

I am shaking a great deal, but the joy and unrest of the past days is too much for me to write nice and comfortably. Just the few lines so that you know that all acquaintances here are well and that our joy will also become yours.

A thousand hearty greetings to all

from your true Henry

Chickasaw Bluffs, the Yazoo Pass Expedition, and the terrible repulse of May 22 had been redeemed; the citadel had fallen.

CHAPTER SIX

"We Should Have Rest"

The marching orders Kircher mentioned in his Independence Day letter quickly put an end to victory celebrations. Despite the siege's success, the Vicksburg campaign had one more phase to unfold. Rebel Gen. Joseph E. Johnston had been building an army at Jackson for weeks, waiting for an opportunity to raise the siege. As soon as Pemberton surrendered, Sherman put plans in motion to deal with this last vestige of organized Confederate strength in western Mississippi.

As part of Sherman's expedition, Kircher's regiment left its intrenchments on July 5 and began one of the most difficult campaigns it experienced. Supply wagons and artillery crowded the Mississippi roads, forcing the soldiers to idle in midsummer heat. They found food rather scarce: "besides our present Generals seem to find great pleasure in seein men and animals drop down sun strock." Fresh water became precious as the Federals found wells along their route polluted by carcasses of cows and hogs. Despite its difficulties, the 12th Missouri reached the earthworks before Jackson on the morning of July 10 and found rest in a peach orchard.[1]

During the next several days, Sherman completed his investment of Jackson. He sparred with its defenders and ordered artillery bombardments while preparing for a regular siege. Grant had ordered him not only to engage Johnston but also to do as much damage to Confederate transportation systems as possible. On July 16, he sent "a good brigade of infantry," Woods's, and a cavalry force toward Canton. Located twenty-five miles north of Jackson, the town contained valuable railroad equipment and maintenance facilities. A short distance beyond, the Mississippi Central Railroad crossed the Big Black River.[2]

Woods's men did their job well. The 12th Missouri helped to pry up track and burn the ties, heating rails over the fire to bend them into worthlessness. The brigade met no serious opposition until the morning of July 17, three miles from Canton. It skirmished with Confederate cavalry and then pushed on, the 12th Missouri in the lead. Heavier fighting occurred at the crossing of Bear Creek.[3]

---

[1] B. H. Liddell Hart, *Sherman: Soldier, Realist, American* (1929; reprint, New York, 1958), 197. Diary, July 5–10, 1863.

[2] *OR*, vol. 24, pt. 2, 535.

[3] Ibid., 618. Diary, July 16–17, 1863.

Camp near Jackson Miss July 22nd 1863

Dear Mother!

On the 15th, our brigade, as well as [Cyrus] Bussey's cavalry (1,500), received the order to go to Canton, 25 miles from here, in order to destroy the railroad and all other government (Confederate) property. Now, what could be more beautiful for us than to see everything go up in flames?

About 3 miles from Canton, the enemy cavalry approached us. We alerted our entire infantry, 5 regiments, 1,500 men, and placed Landgraeber's battery (4 guns) in position. At this moment, about 300 secesh cavalry attacked our left flank and charged our wagon train. In the front, they attempted only a feigned attack. We quickly ordered a gun from the Flying battery and it came just in time to give a hot welcome to the rascals; 12 shells made them fly in all directions and the big battle was over, the victory ours.[4]

We marched with skirmishers in our front to within 2 miles of Canton. There, 2 rifle shots were fired at us, but without hitting anything.

When the skirmishers advanced to Bear Creek, Col. Wangelin and his orderly went onto the bridge and the regiment was to follow, since no further shots were fired. But suddenly, cannon fire and a shell exploded to the left side of his horse, but no harm was done. Now we had to look out. The woods here were very dense and we could not see the enemy. But luckily there was a deep ditch which we (our regiment) used as a rifle pit, while the 2 enemy cannons fired shell after shell, canister after canister at us. We could not return the fire because, first of all, we could not see the enemy, and secondly, our skirmishers were in front and we would have hit them.[5]

Now I was ordered with my company to assist Lieut. [William] Bechtel who, with Company A, was already at the Creek. The cannon fire had stopped and I advanced about 300 yards to reach

---

[4] Clemens Landgraeber commanded the First Horse Artillery, more properly designated Battery F, 2d Missouri Artillery. Kircher's account of the skirmish is essentially accurate, although the 76th Ohio, 25th Iowa, and Bussey's cavalry had as much to do with foiling the Rebel move as did Landgraeber. Kircher's German heritage perhaps excuses his preoccupation with German units. *OR*, vol. 24, pt. 2, 618, 763n.

[5] The Rebel guns were positioned near the end of the bridge. Federal artillery could not return fire because, as Woods put it, "The woods were so dense and the ground so difficult to reconnoiter." Woods also reported that the bridge had been destroyed and the creek crossing obstructed. Ibid., 618–19. In his diary entry of July 17, Kircher explained that the bridge was 300 feet long and had been set afire just before Wangelin tried to cross.

Bechtel. I placed my men behind trees or wherever they could find any protection. Just as we took our positions, rifle shots were fired, but only one hit. Some men tried to go forward but had to retreat again because the enemy fire was too hot. We now fired heavily at our enemy even though we couldn't see them; we had to vent our furies.

Finally after 2 hours, the 3d Missouri succeeded in attacking the enemy in the flank, and they fled in all directions.[6] We stayed where we were all night. The next morning, we marched into Canton and destroyed everything completely and withdrew back 2 miles in the evening.

Our losses were 2 dead and 3 wounded. The 3d Missouri also lost 2 dead. We have heard that the enemy was 3–4,000 men strong and we had only 3,000. Furthermore, they had such a good position, and if they would have done a better job we would never have been able to cross the creek. In the evening, we heard that Jackson with 13 heavy guns and 5–600 prisoners was captured.[7]

A thousand greetings to all of you.

Your loyal Henry

On July 18, Canton, "a quite pleasant town, wide spread, most houses having gardens in front," became an inferno.[8] All of Woods's infantry set about the work of destruction. Railroad tracks, locomotives, cars, engine house, repair and machine shops, depots, offices, and two miles of rails "burned and bent" represented the day's accomplishments. Bussey's cavalry rode north to burn the trestle over Big Black, fulfilling Grant's instructions to Sherman. That evening, the Federals marched back to Bear Creek for a night bivouac.[9] Kircher noted that many Canton residents followed the troops south, afraid of the Rebels' return. The Southerners "had Killed a doctor day before our arrival there, he having opposed their ploundering." Negroes in the area also sought the Yankees and were "strewen allong the

---

[6] To force a crossing, Woods ordered the 12th and 17th Missouri to hold the Rebels near the bridge by demonstrations. He also sent the 3d Missouri to cross the creek by any means available. They did so and advanced through a cornfield to drive the enemy away. Woods then ordered the 12th Missouri to cross Bear Creek "under and to the right of the bridge, which was done." *OR*, vol. 24, pt. 2, 619.

[7] Kircher's report of losses in the 3d and 12th Missouri coincides exactly with Woods's report. Woods learned that Rebel strength at Bear Creek totaled 2,000 and Bussey reported that his cavalry and Woods's infantry combined also numbered 2,000. Jackson fell to Sherman on July 17, with 400 prisoners. Ibid., 528, 552, 619. The news of Jackson's capture reached Woods's brigade on the evening of July 18, as recorded by Kircher in his diary.

[8] Diary, July 18, 1863.

[9] *OR*, vol. 24, pt. 2, 619.

whole road." The brigade continued its march southward on July 19 and reached Jackson early the next morning.[10]

The regiment lay in camp for three days. With Johnston's army driven east, there remained little to do but see the sights. Kircher visited Jackson on July 22 and reported "rather sad scenery, All stores, publick houses (except State and Court house) manufactories and some few dwelling houses have been consumed by the flames, partially through federal as well as conferate hands [.] Many citizens leave for Vicksburg or the north. The rebs will see into there folly by and by, and play quits, for conquered they will and must be, last it 100 years."[11]

On the same day, he longingly wrote home: "Now we eagerly wait for a marching order, which should arrive today or tomorrow. Sherman circulated an order that Johnston and his army are dispersed and are pushing to Meridian and that our summer expedition is finished, and we all have to march to Vicksburg and stay there or wherever?! We need to take a rest from our fatigues. Maybe I will be able to visit you, where I surely would be able to recover from my fatigue (which really did not harm me). I hope [Sherman] can see this and will let me go?!"[12]

The regiment began its retrograde march on July 23. It reached the Big Black River two days later, but not without delay caused by snarled traffic. Kircher waited for three hours at a crossroads while Gen. Hugh Ewing's 3d Brigade, 2d Division, 15th Corps took the right of way. "In fact we were on the cross road first with our reimt. but G. [Ewing] had played a not quite worthy trick for a General, in sending a few ambulances an hour march ahead of his column to the crossroad and thereby claimed to be the first on the road. Our being commanded by a Col. but a Gentleman, we were pushed aside." The regiment moved to its assigned campsite on July 28 and prepared for a long rest.[13]

Camp near Black R. R. R. Bridge
July 29th 1863

Dear Mother!

I wanted to write you yesterday, but a heavy rain (we haven't had any tents since Vicksburg) held me up. But the weather is fair again today and since my Louis (Negro) is finished building my leaf hut I can write you a few lines sitting comfortably on a half empty wine box.

Finally, after the craziest, stupidest marches (always in the

---

[10] Diary, July 18, 1863.
[11] Diary, July 22, 1863.
[12] This is the last paragraph of Kircher's preceding July 22 letter.
[13] Diary, July 23, 25, 28, 1863.

noonday sun) that I have ever experienced, we arrived here. Uncle knows the place, about 1 or 1½ miles from General Osterhaus's house that he had for headquarters when Uncle and I visited him along the railroad that goes to Vicksburg.

Whether we can stay here long one can only speculate. We hear that our army corps is supposed to go down the Mississippi to Natchez to take summer quarters. By all means we should have rest, and it might be possible for me to get a leave, probably just short, but long enough to visit you. We can't really speak of getting thoroughly rested because we have all our tents, articles of clothing, etc., in Vicksburg, but everything is supposed to arrive tomorrow. You can imagine what a tremendous pleasure it was yesterday noon when we suddenly came across Bert Affleck and Lieut. Seipel.[14] They looked very good and are in good spirits.

A thousand greetings from all acquaintances and friends.

Your true son Henry

For the next several days, the regiment concerned itself with the important task of making its camp as comfortable as possible. Tents arrived from Vicksburg on July 30. That day, Captain Ferdinand Steinberg of Company K rejoined the 12th Missouri after convalescing from his hip injury on May 22. His presence on duty prompted Kircher to apply for a twenty-day leave of absence. Higher authorities approved it on August 4, but Kircher waited more than a week before leaving.[15]

In the meantime, he was sent on regimental business to Vicksburg. Traveling by railroad to buy vegetables for the men, he took time to look at the town that had held out so long against Federal efforts. It was his first visit to the historic place. "The heat was so intens, I could but have a glims at a part of the rebel works, but sufficient to prove the strength and almost imposibility to take them by storm. Most Guns are removed. the shelling did not as much damage to the houses as I had expected, although pieces of shells are strewen all over the streets and yards. Artificial caves of considerable size were very numerous, dug during the siege. Courthouse had one Piller at the Couples, almost cut through by a Ball of some of our Parots. other wise it has a few more marks of shells and ball, but no serious damage don. One mortar shell had also entered at the top and passed to the bottom.

---

[14] Affleck and Henry Seipel rejoined the regiment after long sick leaves to recover from their May 22 wounds. Muster rolls, Albert Affleck and Henry Seipel service records, NA. In his diary entry of July 28, Kircher described them "as heardy and gay as ever, Rally round the Flag Boys! & ct. ct."

[15] Diary, July 30, 31, Aug. 4, 1863.

Almost every house in the city has been strock by one or more balls, but in but few instances it has toren down houses. at some houses the mortar shell ha[ve] passed clear through from top to bottom. all streets running in an angle with the river were baricaded by strong breast works for Artillery. their guns had been of all kinds and sizes as the yet scattered projectiles show."[16]

Kircher and Capt. William Mittmann of Company C spent the next day "running around a good deal for vegitables . . . being only partly successful." He gave up and "left with afternoon train for camp, being heartily tired of the virgin city Vicksb." Mittmann rejoined the regiment on August 9 with the necessary produce.[17]

Finally, on August 12, Kircher received a pass to proceed on his leave of absence. He left for Vicksburg on the morning of August 13, taking a supply of cane so his uncle could make a southern-style bench for a garden. In the river town, he learned that the *Sultana* was scheduled to steam upriver. Kircher deposited his baggage and visited the army hospital with Casimir Andel, who returned to camp after escorting his friend on the first leg of his journey home. Kircher spent the night, accompanied by a swarm of Mississippi mosquitoes, with an acquaintance who served as a government aid aboard the steamer *Swan*.[18]

The next day, Kircher began a comic game of roulette when he learned that the *Sultana* had changed its destination and intended steaming downriver. The *Sunshine*, however, was due to go in his direction. He paid a fifteen-dollar fare and hurried his baggage to her landing; too late, as it turned out, for the boat was already puffing away in mid-stream when he arrived. "I was left, a good joak." Word came that the *White Cloud* was due to travel north. Kircher put his bags aboard, squeezing among the many passengers who had already secured a spot on the boat. His troubles were far from over, for a half hour before her scheduled departure time authorities ordered the *White Cloud* downriver.[19]

After a day almost as trying as any battle, Kircher sought a place to spend the night. The *Swan* had by then left Vicksburg, so he stayed with another acquaintance, a clerk in the Commissary Department. On August 15, he made another try at a berth. The *Luminary* reportedly planned to go north, so he stowed his baggage for the fourth time to be ready early the next morning.[20]

---

[16] For several months in 1863, Kircher kept a second copy of his diary entries. The quotation is a fusion of both copies of his Aug. 7 entry. Throughout, the two copies differ insubstantially.

[17] Diary, Aug. 8, 9, 1863.

[18] Diary, Aug. 12, 13, 1863.

[19] Diary, Aug. 14, 1863.

[20] Diary, Aug. 15, 1863.

Having friends in the Commissary Department paid well. Kircher ate a "good breakfast" on the morning of August 16 and confidently expected to put Vicksburg behind him. It proved to be a difficult task. After boarding the *Luminary* at 10 A.M., he learned she was, instead, going south. Again, word arrived of another boat's imminent departure upriver. The *Hannibal* was packed with people who were probably as frustrated as Kircher, "but being determined to go with first boat, I crowded in." The boat left at 1 P.M., steaming at last in the right direction; "Glory glory hallahuja," recorded the jubilant lieutenant.[21]

The journey was not easy. Kircher learned that 1,200 passengers were crowded aboard the boat, which rendered sleeping arrangements difficult and food a precious commodity. Four or five people sat at each table and, although he found the fare "poor," Kircher had "almost to fight for eatables." A six-hour delay ensued when the *Hannibal* ran onto a sandbar below Memphis, but the dinner stop at that city allowed many passengers to debark. The boat struck another sandbar before arriving at Cairo at 2 A.M., August 21. There, Kircher struggled to secure tickets on the 3:30 A.M. train to O'Fallon; as at Vicksburg, many soldiers longed eagerly for a quick visit to their homes. He arrived at one o'clock that afternoon and rode to Belleville with an acquaintance.[22]

Although he did not write of his ten-day visit, Kircher found pleasure in once again seeing his home. On August 31, he went to St. Louis to book passage south. He left two days later, "Clinging fast to the last glims of the great Queen of the West, St. Louis, while my mind was wandering once more to Belleville pondering when Fortune would once again ga[r]land my steps thither!" When they reached Cairo the next day, Kircher spent his spare time drinking wine and sightseeing.[23]

Board Steamer *Champion* September 3rd 63

Dear Mother!

Our trip so far was quite good, just the beginning was slow. But why should this be an exception, since all beginnings are difficult? Instead of Monday, the boat didn't leave until 1 P.M. on Wednesday [September 2]. If the clerk had simply told me this, then I would have been with you for 1 or 2 days, but as always "this morning, this afternoon, positively in 2 hours," and so on.

I brought Uncle and Loulou as far as the cars, and ate lunch with Uncle, all the other Bellevillers in a circle.[24] Since Uncle told

---

[21] Diary, Aug. 16, 1863.

[22] Diary, Aug. 17, 19, 20, 21, 1863.

[23] Diary, Aug. 31, Sept. 2, 3, 1863.

[24] Goedeking and Loulou were on their way to a political meeting in Springfield. Diary, Sept. 1, 1863.

me the picture of me from Neff was quite worse than an ape, I wanted to get a picture taken by Hoelke and Beneke. I couldn't because the boat was sure to leave at 10.

We are all healthy and in good spirits. Hearty greetings to all.

Your son Henry

Steamer Champion September 6th 63

Dear Mother!

At night we seldom travel, since our ship is heavily loaded and the river so low. Still, better slow and definite than to get completely stuck.

Already, we have gotten about half a ship's length above the sand. But with "full steam" we made it, with gasping, puffing and crashing, the way a snake winds his way over it. Twice we have had to set the horses (about 50–70) on land and let them march a few miles to lighten the ship. Today, it's 2 days over my leave and probably 2 more will be added to that, then it will be 4, if there is no misfortune.

As I see in the papers of the 4th, Uncle delivered a speech in Springfield. At least it said "Hon. H. Goodeking." Who else can that be but the X mayor of Belleville?[25] The boat has peculiar rules; it must not know that there is a war going on. Today, it forbids card playing because it's Sunday. That doesn't break me up because I never play, but today I would really like to. If a person goes to hell at an early time for that reason, that is my look out.[26]

As you see, I am quite well. I always think the [remaining] year will go faster the sooner I enter my service. Therefore, I am ready to rejoin the regiment and get back to you that much sooner.

Anyway, I believe things are quite shaky for the South. It will soon lie in ruins and beg for mercy. Many hearty greetings to all.

Your faithful son Henry

---

[25] Union supporters in Illinois held a mass meeting on the Springfield fairgrounds to counterbalance an earlier meeting of state Democrats. Newspapers proclaimed it "one of the most successful love feasts that has ever come off in the West." Illinois Germans also gathered to hear the "Hon. H. Goodking of St. Clair county," as well as others. They passed resolutions reaffirming their support for the war effort and for slavery's abolition. *Chicago Daily Tribune,* Sept. 4, 1863.

[26] Kircher expressed himself more sarcastically in his diary entry of September 6. Denied cards, he spent the day reading and sleeping. "It seems very funny to see men take so much interest, according to their notion, in our welfare, they thinking it sinfull to play cards on Sunday[;] what business is it if I want to go to hell, it's a free Count[r]y."

Camp near Bovina, Miss Sept. 10th 63

Dear Mother!

Yesterday evening, we arrived well preserved and cheerful in Vicksburg and this morning I went to the camp on the Big Black, found all acquaintances well and cheerful. Casimir was the first one to see me and to repay my hearty handshake, Bert the next. Bert is now the provost marshal of our division. General Osterhaus, whom I visited and found well, commands our division.[27] I was received quite heartily and friendly by all, and why not? We have been comrades through joy and sorrow for 2 years already.

The health of the troops, although not very good, is still considerably better than a month ago—mostly fever and diarrhea. But yellow fever, as the newspapers are prattling about, is out of the question.

Did Uncle and Loulou arrive safely home from the tumult and appear back in the friendly family circle? Or are they still quaffing the patriotic extract of the great lion of the Fatherland? Aren't the cowardly men and copperheads trembling yet? Then we would have to give a frolic and let the sick bay speak. The lot of such dogs is to kick the bucket. Why not grant it to them?

My heartiest greetings to all.

Your faithful Henry

On the evening of September 10, the day of his return to the regimental family, Kircher received his commission as captain in the volunteer army. It arrived as part of a wide distribution of honors for the good work performed at Vicksburg. Casimir Andel was promoted to first lieutenant, Fred Tell Ledergerber to major, and Anthony Engelmann to captain. Kircher mustered into his new rank on September 12 and took command of Company E the next day.[28]

Camp Sherman
near Black River Miss. Sept 12th 1863

Dear Father!

It was terribly necessary, upon my installation as Captain of Company E, not to let it go by quite so terribly dry. Namely, Major Ledergerber, Capt. Engelmann and I decided to give a jolly evening to our friends, since we all rose one rank. We invited General Osterhaus and appendages (staff), Major from the 3d Mo., Captains Schuster and [Otto C.] Lademann [of the 3d Missouri], as well as

---

[27] Osterhaus resumed command of his old division on September 1.
[28] Diary, Sept. 10, 12, 13, 1863.

all officers of the [12th Missouri] regiment: served strawberry and pineapple punch, Belleville gingerbread (Miss Ledergerber's manufacture), "segars," later lunch as well. They were all quite lively, let live and lived. General Osterhaus gave the toast after we let him live as a Major General; "May every person in the party be assembled around me and have attained his stars by the time the war is over."[29] But there was general agreement that it would be better to let the war end earlier, for otherwise it would become a Thirty Years War.

After midnight, we disbanded to spend the rest of the night in peace. Since there were also 4 new 1st lieutenants, their pride will probably cherish a desire for a ceremony too.

The commissions from the Governor of Missouri are also different than usual. On top, above the eagle, is written "For gallant conduct during the actions at Vicksburg," in red ink. It irritated the old ones somewhat, but pleased us all the more.

The condition of health, in the regiment particularly, is getting better daily. We have only 50 sick. Overall, in the short time that Osterhaus has been commanding us, there is order and cleaner camps than before, etc., which all contributes a lot toward good health.

The secesh say that Fort Wagner as well as the entire island is in our possession.[30] Good and believable news, it comes from the enemy.

Many hearty greetings to all.

Your obedient Henry

Camp Sherman Miss. September 22nd 1863

Dear Mother!

For a few days it has been so cool here, downright cold, this morning too. My fingers are quite stiff on me; therefore it will be some effort to read my letter.

Yesterday, we, our brigade, made an expedition.[31] At 11 P.M.

---

[29] Osterhaus was still a brigadier general at that time.

[30] Fort Wagner was a bastion that formed part of the defenses of Charleston, South Carolina. It and all of Morris Island fell to Federal troops on Sept. 7.

[31] Acting on a report that 6,000 Rebel infantry were on their way to attack Vicksburg, Sherman planned to send cavalry on a reconnoitering expedition. At the last moment, he learned from a reliable source that the report was untrue but ordered the cavalry out anyway. Col. Edward F. Winslow led 15th Corps horsemen toward Auburn and Cayuga on Sept. 21. On the same day, Osterhaus took Woods's brigade toward Raymond to cover Winslow's movements. *OR*, vol. 30, pt. 3, 735, 748–49.

[September 20], came the order to be ready at 4 A.M. with one day's rations to march yesterday, as I said. With General Osterhaus at the head it went forward, and since it was brisk, everybody gave his legs full rein. In 3½ hours we were at the spot, 10 miles from our camp. We went scouting for our cavalry, who left the evening before. Finally, at 12 o'clock, they came, covered with dust and some without any head covering. Some [Rebels] had absconded and our boys painted the picture in the brightest colors of how it must have gone. They had gotten 3 prisoners; maybe just a few poor Hushers that they had made the objects of their courage, since they didn't get or want anything to do with the enemy.[32]

Now it went up and away from there. Our regiment was in back and therefore now in front. Lieut. Bechtel of Comp. B, the first commander, took off now with a step that resembled that of a camel in the desert when it gets in a hurry.[33] It wasn't doing anything, it was going home; and the sooner we got there the sooner we got to rest. Around 3 o'clock, we passed General Osterhaus's headquarters with the sound of drums and bugles. He was not a little pleased that his old regiment marched so well and left all the others far behind. You can believe that we were able to sleep well that night, for 20 miles in 6½ hours of marching is not such a very little bitty trifle. But if you're healthy and willing, anything goes.

If only Meade will dare and attack Lee energetically.[34] The rebels are defeated by their own persuasion and are just wrestling in their last death throes. If we just risk it and not wait until something can happen that will revive their sunken spirit. Once troops are defeated in their morale it is also easy to give them a sound black-and-blue beating physically.

Many hearty greetings to all who take an interest in me; may the rest climb on my back and break their necks.

Your true Henry

As he wrote his September 22 letter, Kircher could look back on a summer's rest disturbed only by the jaunt to Raymond. Far to the east on

[32] Osterhaus marched nearly to Raymond but neither he nor Winslow found any substantial Confederate forces. They captured three Rebel scouts: a captain, a lieutenant, and a sergeant. Ibid., 758.

[33] After the Jackson-Canton Expedition, Bechtel was transferred to Company B. Muster rolls, William Bechtel service record, NA.

[34] Following Gettysburg on July 1–3, 1863 and before the Mine Run Campaign of November, 1863, George G. Meade's Army of the Potomac and Robert E. Lee's Army of Northern Virginia engaged in no significant movements.

that day, other Federal soldiers huddled in a small Tennessee town walled by mountains and ridges while they recovered from the shock of one of the war's worst battles. Their defeat caused repercussions all the way to the Big Black River; a day or two later, Kircher began what proved to be his last campaign.

CHAPTER SEVEN

"They Have Paid Their Obligation"

The movement that drew Kircher from his comfortable Mississippi home was the brainchild of Gen. William S. Rosecrans. More than a week before Vicksburg's surrender, he started his Army of the Cumberland on a campaign that cleared most of southeastern Tennessee of Rebels. In August, he drove deeper into the Confederacy, maneuvered Braxton Bragg's Army of Tennessee out of Chattanooga, and pursued it into the wilds of northern Georgia. Reinforced by both western and eastern Confederates, Bragg turned on the Cumberlanders and brought off a stunning victory at Chicka-mauga on September 19 and 20. Rosecrans's crippled army retreated to Chattanooga, where Bragg tried to starve it into submission with a siege.[1]

The Federal defeat brought responses from both theaters of war. Two corps from Meade's Army of the Potomac hurried westward over the rails while Sherman's 15th Corps geared up for a long journey via river and road. Osterhaus's division led the corps' departure from the Big Black.

Board *Sam Gatz* Sept. 26th 1863

Dear Mother!

My last letter was one day before our departure from Camp Sherman.[2] Of course, at that time I didn't know anything about it. It didn't arrive until the morning of the day of our breaking camp [September 22], the order for the whole Osterhaus division to be ready to march at 4 P.M. with sack and pack. At 5:00, we were on the way to Vicksburg and the next morning [September 23] we were there. At 11:00, we were already on the *New Sam Gatz* with all our baggage and hodgepodge. It puffed one cloud of steam after the other toward heaven, making its way upstream through the great Father of all Rivers. Last night at 10, we went past Napoleon and now we are still 60–70 miles from Helena, where we will probably arrive at noon today.

It was amusing all day when we had received the order until we marched. There was general joy and there were outbursts of sat-

---

[1] B. H. Liddell Hart, *Sherman: Soldier, Realist, American* (1929; reprint, New York, 1958), 210–11.
[2] Kircher's diary indicates that the division left the Big Black River encampments on the twenty-second, the same day he wrote his preceding letter.

isfaction and pleasure during the day at being able finally to move again, which more resembled a hellish noise than cries of delight. Everybody wanted to know where we were going but nobody knew. We could only speculate. Most believed we were going to Galveston, Matamoras or somewhere else in the southern part of Texas.[3] Some believed we would have to make another pleasure trip to Ste. Genevieve to recuperate. Others believe we are going to Rosecrans. The latter ones will be right, in my opinion, although I can also only guess.

This is the way it goes with soldiers, all content in their souls to march: where to? It doesn't matter at all. Wherever the Red One (Osterhaus) can go, we can go too. And we know that there will be rags there. What else does a soldier want? Forward march!

But I know this is not sufficient for you. However, I can't give you any more information from the front. The assurance that General Osterhaus will lead us wherever we are going satisfies me. I assure you of it and you will be satisfied too.

In Vicksburg, the regiment laid in about 100 boxes of wine to illuminate our departure from the Virgin City. Each company had about 5 or 6 boxes and we had only 30 dozen Laubenseiner, Düdesfelder and also red wine for punch. You can imagine our journey is not wasted nor very boring. Besides, we get the wine at St. Louis cost prices, 8–10 dollars. Our mess committee took care of snacks. And so we are experiencing quite happy days. Who knows when we will run into it again?

It is remarkable weather. There are always a few cool (almost cold) days, then the full heat springs up again. Do you have this too? But despite everything, I feel as well and strong and self-content as ever. At least all my comrades claim I must have undergone some kind of magic in B[elleville], that I have never been so jolly.

Many greetings to all.

Your true son Henry

The division reached Memphis on September 27 and camped east of town for two days. As Kircher recorded searchingly in his diary, his mood suddenly changed from self-confident to melancholy, introspective, doubtful. An event that changed his life still lay two months in the future, but his

---

[3] The 13th Corps had been ordered to the lower Mississippi in early August to report to Banks, providing a precedent for speculation that Sherman's troops might follow. *OR*, vol. 24, pt. 3, 581.

vague uneasiness foreshadowed it with a novelist's touch of expectation.[4] "It is warm, cloudy and sultry and the air seems to be presing very heavy on a man's chest. Is it than the weather the air or what is it, that makes me feel lonesome, miscontent, sad, tired Oh' awfull. It is no [illness], I did not drink a gill of any liquer since we left the boat, have not been to Memphis yet, dont feel inclined to go there, although so many go and say they enjoy it. why not try it too[.] yes I will go this evening, it may liven me up[.] it is better than [to] sit in the tent and trying to read or think of happy day. Oh yes[,] happy-happy days[;] that is it they have vanished[.] will they return[?] what a question[,] why should they not?—

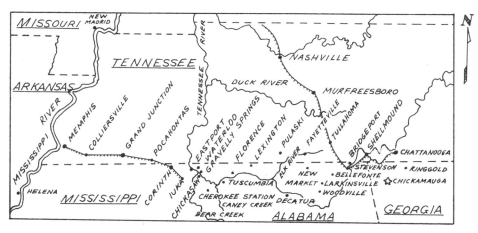

The Chattanooga campaign

"But still something is troubling my mind[.] is it an Ohmen of something to come, Is there anything like forefeeling?—Still nothing, nothing tells me of danger or sade news from my beloved at home.—

"May come what will, can I change natures course? I will endeavor to stand up and beare like a man[.] yes[,] how I know father, the example of all men that have a right to that name, wants me [to] act . . . it shall be done.

> In the world's brand field of battle,
> In the bivouac of life;
> Be not like dumb driven cattle
> Be a hero in the strife.

These few words from Longfellow[,] they please me so few and what *do* they express? or better what *don't* they comprise?"

Camp near Memphis Tenn September 29th 1863
Dear Mother!
You will not be a little surprised to suddenly receive a letter

---

[4] Diary, Sept. 27, 29, 1863.

from me from this direction. God's ways are mighty and those of a soldier are *fl*ighty!

Would I serve if we got involved in a war with France and Mexico? Time must tell and show. If I really am supposed to answer that, I would really not be a soldier any more today or tomorrow. I will be heartily happy when the 10 months are finally up, although I am again sworn for 3 years from the date of receiving my commission and would (if one couldn't resign) still have 3, or 5 in all, to serve. According to a new order, everyone who advances to a newly received rank is mustered in for 3 years from the time when he received his commission. As long as this is not done, he can't draw any pay or take advantage of his rank. So there was nothing left for me to do but to hold my hand up to heaven until I heard "so help you God," put my papers away, say "adieu," and to walk away as Capt. was the whole situation. And if the regiment is mustered out before the 3 years are up what are they going to do with all the officers? They would also have to be mustered out. I'm not going to let myself get any gray hairs about it. What you make up your mind to do you can do, even get out of the service and still sleep honorably at night. I don't want it any other way. Another page, another subject.

I haven't been able to find out anything more than that we are supposed to go to Corinth or Clear Creek, both on the railroad. The 9th Illinois is at Pocahontas [Tennessee]. I might get to see Mersy too.

You wrote in your letter that I was so quiet when I was with you. Did I ever show my satisfaction and pleasure to others with crazy jumps for joy and roaring?

I am quite alive and well, as are all acquaintances too.

Your Henry

The movement east continued on September 29. That afternoon, the regiment marched to the railroad depot and loaded its baggage aboard the cars. Rain fell all day, giving Kircher "a strong chill and fever." He ate his supper late and tried, with other regimenters, to sleep on the depot's hard floor. On the next day, September 30, steaming locomotives pulled the troops to Corinth. Kircher felt better as he set up his tent near the depot, but the illness returned on October 1. "Every bone feels broken[,] every [sinew] strained awfull—fever[.] Took Quinine by the bushel and sent a chimeny sweep down my bowels."[5]

---

[5] Diary, Sept. 30, Oct. 1, 2, 3, 1863.

When the 12th Missouri marched to its campsite at a fortification on College Hill on October 2, Kircher rode in an ambulance. For eight days, the regiment remained near Corinth while logistical arrangements for the whole of Sherman's force were worked out. The wait allowed Kircher to describe his illness in letters home.[6]

Camp in Fort College Hill
near Corinth Miss. October 6th 1863

Dear Father!

[On] Oct. 1, I still felt sick in the morning and got strong laxative from the doctor, which made me very weak and kaputt but was very good. The headache let up. On the next day, Oct. 2, we removed our camp to 1½ miles northwest of Corinth. This was the *first* time that I went in an ambulance during a march and I hope the last time. But I wouldn't have been able to have walked that far. Now we pitched the tents and I consumed quinine as needed and felt better too, and got a whole bunch of fever blisters around my mouth. But on the next day I was able to write; sat in quarterly, monthly, etc. returns up to my ears, which all have to be in Washington inside 30 days. Otherwise they play "stop the pay," and that is supposed to be most unpleasant.

Well into this evening, I got finished. And then we are supposed to move again tomorrow, 3 miles farther, to Clear Creek. So I must write yet tonight or it will delay even longer.

I am quite well again, only the decorations on my nose and mouth embarrass me very much.

Greeting everybody cordially, I remain

your most obedient son Henry

Camp near Corinth
Clear Creek October 9th 1863

Dear Mother!

Again, just as we are ready to march off, a dear letter from you surprised me, dated October 1st. It was this morning at 8 o'clock and as we got new rifles, we received a counter order and aren't marching until tomorrow.[7] As far as I could learn, to Iuka and then on to Tuscumbia, both on the Memphis-Charleston R.R. I also be-

---

[6] Diary, Oct. 3, 11, 1863.
[7] After it received the marching order, the 12th Missouri made ready to go. Higher authorities, however, delayed its departure so the men could exchange their old arms for "poor second handed polished up Enfield Muskets." Diary, Oct. 9, 1863.

lieve that will be our (15th Army C.) destination, at least temporarily. Perhaps after 2–3 months we will push on to Rosecrans. However, I can't imagine that we would provide reinforcements, as is generally rumored, because we would have the very farthest distance (200 miles on land, *per pedes*). Fourteen days of persistant marching might bring us there, assuming the enemy would put no stumbling blocks in our way. So "reinforcing," which would also be much too late, is in my opinion just hot air.

We are "in great distress" if we now go on the march. For every 2 companies there is only one wagon. We used to have 2 wagons to one company. In officers, 2 to a company, one tent. Luckily, we now have only 1 officer in each company. Joe L[edergerber] and I are together in a wall tent.

When we went past Pocahontas, where the 9th is, I didn't see anything of Mersy. He is supposed to have been sick recently. G. Osterhaus had visited him and said he didn't snap his fingers any more as he used to do when something didn't go according to his wishes; but he pulled his coattail through his right hand and held it up in the air representing a donkey's ear. Very meaningful?

Now, the friendliest greetings to all.

Lively and loyal, your Henry

(Paix de Coeur)

The 12th Missouri remained at Corinth one more night, October 9. Kircher's sleep was bothered by a dream, possibly inspired by his recent illness and the death of an army acquaintance by disease. "Conjistive Chills" killed his friend, a Lieutenant Piduck; "so it is [,] those that are spared by bullets may still fall in the cold clutches of death."[8] Kircher's own dreamworld demise was much less gloomy. "I thought I was very sick but had no pains [;] was at home, and All seemed to give me up. I asked as last wish (M.S.) to let me gaze at her while in the same costume as Eve while she was in Paradise. She complied and I died. How foolish a person dreams."[9]

Dark nightmares plagued another 12th Missourian, Kircher's close friend Casimir Andel. The battles and their consequences intruded into his sleep. "Casimir dreamt several times already that he had a leg amputated. He thinks the next fight or battle we have will cost one of his legs. I hope not."[10]

Kircher's unit resumed the long march eastward on October 10 and rejoined its division that afternoon. Osterhaus pushed on across the rough

---

[8] Piduck did not serve in the 12th Missouri and his regiment is unknown. Diary, Oct. 8, 1863.

[9] Diary, Oct. 10, 1863. The identity of M. S. is unknown.

[10] Diary, Oct. 10, 1863.

terrain of northern Mississippi and Alabama, made even more bleak by two years of war. "The country here is rather like southern Mo. hilly, stony and san[d]y," Kircher recorded, "not furtil at all. cripled timbre and mighty Pines Oaks and Chessnuts a strewen over hills and dales[.] water plenty[,] nice and clear."[11]

The towns presented a sight that was barely more pleasing. Brownsville was "almost deserted," with only a few troops to occupy its "1 or 2 dozen of houses." Engineers had extended the railroad to within two miles of Iuka, where Osterhaus's division rested from October 11 until the seventeenth. Kircher could do little but gloomily record the rainfall in his diary and occasionally escort a foraging party. Few farmers worked the poor land and foraging wagons returned only half full. The regiment also practiced firing its Enfields. From near Collierville, Tennessee, came word that Confederate guerrillas almost captured corps commander Sherman on October 11. "It would be a sore joke for us," Kircher thought.[12]

With cool, clear weather above them, the Federals marched six miles east of Iuka to Big Bear Creek. Half a dozen guerrillas, "coward hounds" Kircher called them, fired into a Union camp and fled. They portended more serious fighting to come. On the nineteenth, U.S. paymasters doled out to the company leaders their soldiers' pay. Kircher distributed the money to his charges next morning, just before the eastward advance continued.[13]

On that day, October 20, Osterhaus's division marched eight miles via Dickson's Station to Cherokee Station, Alabama. Advanced Federal cavalry skirmished sporadically with Rebel horsemen, capturing a few. At 7:30 P.M., orders arrived to march forward rapidly to reinforce the 5th Ohio Cavalry, which skirmished sharply with Jeffrey E. Forrest's cavalry near Barton's Station. With bright moonlight showing the way, the 12th Missouri covered the six to seven miles in two hours. The danger was no longer imminent, so Kircher and his fellow regimenters bivouacked for the night.[14]

The weather disrupted all plans for rest. Rain began to fall at 2 A.M., "spattering away at my Rubber cloth as if it was determined to Knock holes in." A toothache added to Kircher's discomfort. He gave up sleep and stood by the fire until daylight. Osterhaus had planned to advance his division to that forward post by morning, but his superiors ordered him to stay at Cherokee Station. The 12th Missouri then marched back; "that was fun, wet, still reining, muddy, slippery, Knap sack soked with water on the back[.] but little rest, and to crown all[,] no breakfast."

The picket, two 5th Ohio Cavalry companies, followed the regiment back; so did the Rebels. Soon after Kircher settled into a much-needed rest,

---

[11] Diary, Oct. 10, 11, 1863.
[12] Diary, Oct. 11–13, 16, 1863.
[13] Diary, Oct. 17–20, 1863.
[14] Diary, Oct. 20, 1863. *OR*, vol. 31, pt. 1, 17.

the enemy attacked the Federal pickets at noon, October 21. A sharp fight ensued with casualties on both sides, but the 12th Missouri missed the action. After maneuvering within supporting distance all afternoon, Kircher returned to his bed. "It is almost nonsense to say that I soon slept like a bear after eating like a wolf." The regiment rested at Cherokee on October 22 and 23, giving Kircher an opportunity to tell the folks at home of his adventures.[15]

Camp near Cherokee Station Alabama
October 23rd 1863

Dear Uncle [Goedeking]!

Although we don't carry on a frequent correspondence, I still know that a letter from this corner is welcome anyway. I have wanted to write you for a long time to congratulate you on your oratorical talent (it must be considerable, or I wouldn't have seen your name among our chief speakers at the Springfield convention), and to obtain the contents or a copy of the speech.

I am very sorry that I didn't go with you and Loulou, especially when I learned in Cairo that I could have come back early enough to go downstream with our boat.

Certainly there was an assembly of loyal citizens gathered there in great numbers, and they all felt their patriotic, joyful hearts beating strongly and free again in their chests. For when so many upright, honest and brave people appear, a scoundrel and traitor feels the ground shake under his pitiful sulphur matches and, no longer sure of his omnipotence, he vanishes.

But what does the enormous draft of 300,000 volunteers and 800,000 conscripts mean? "How are you conscript, how are you today?!" "A little shaky, my belly hurts me so!" will be sung by so many who thought they were safe. Yesterday evening, a rumor of this draft came from headquarters. Nobody knows anything definite about it yet.[16] Now, I will tell you about our latest pastimes and jokes.

On the 19th of this month, we marched to Bear Creek, camped for the night and during the same were paid for July and August, which lasted until 2 in the morning. I didn't take any

---

[15] Diary, Oct. 21, 1863. *OR*, vol. 31, pt. 1, 17.

[16] On Oct. 17, 1863, Lincoln issued a call for 300,000 volunteers to serve three years. The rumored draft occurred on Feb. 1, 1864 and required a total of 500,000 men, including the earlier drafts in 1863, to serve three years. Francis A. Lord, *They Fought for the Union* (Harrisburg, Pa., 1960), 6.

money, as there was an error in the payroll and I would have had to forfeit $30–$40. So I have my months of May, June, July, August, September and October ($740) coming on the next payday, a tidy little sum.

After surviving this, we marched about 8–9 miles from 8 A.M. until noon [October 20] to this place, Cherokee Station, 15 miles from Tuscumbia. Our wagons arrived at 1 P.M., and an hour later we devoured with great appetites our bacon and beans in our numerous tents. All day long, our avant garde (5th Ohio Cavalry and 1 battalion of 3d Regular Cavalry), altogether 800 men, kept having to drive away enemy cavalry (Forrest) from in front of them. Here and there they had a small skirmish with them, but insignificant, as the 5th Ohio would have taken care of the enemy without regulars. The result was that we received 2 dead and 5 wounded, the enemy about the same; but besides that, there was a captain and 5 men that we took prisoner.[17]

—I stopped here because Col. Kaercher and Lieut. Bechtel arrived, brought me the letters and tobacco, and I was invited to a punch at the doctor's and could inquire about Belleville.[18] I thought I could finish it this morning, but listen:

October 24th. The prisoners were the last thing I mentioned. Now, at 7:30 in the evening [October 20], when we had just gotten in bed, tired from the day's march, there came an order for our regiment to appear momentarily and to march 7 miles farther, where our cavalry (5th Ohio) and 2 cannons were. At 9:30, we arrived there, still tired of course, and lay on our blankets and soon got to sleep. But at 2 o'clock in the morning [October 21] it started to rain, and we had to spend the 4 hours until break of day in the rain, wrapped up in our poncho blankets.

At 7 A.M., we got the order to march back to the camp of yesterday, which we finally accomplished by noon despite the mud and the rain, with empty stomachs. Our [baggage] wagons were loaded, and we had to pitch our tents again in the mud. That was hardly done when we moved into the tents, longing for a bed, and we had the Negroes bring the food to us. I stretched out in bed and said sarcastically to Joe Ledergerber, "I only wish that our pickets had

---

[17] Osterhaus reported that the 5th Ohio Cavalry lost one mortally and three slightly wounded that day. Of the Rebels, two dead, four wounded, and five prisoners fell into Federal hands. *OR*, vol. 31, pt. 1, 17.

[18] Bechtel had just returned from a leave home. Muster rolls, William Bechtel service record, NA.

been attacked and we had to march out of here," so that the story would be capped off right with a crown!

Then our pickets fired merrily, and in all nooks and crannies the alarm went thundering out. Jumping out of bed, reporting and welcoming the enemy on the spot was our pleasure for a few minutes. It was still raining. Now it turned out that there were about 2,000 cavalry and mounted infantry who made a sharp attack, to be sure, because they must have thought that it was just the 2 regiments, the 12th Missouri and the 5th Ohio Cavalry, with two 12-pound howitzers which were now standing in their way. Their intention was to frighten us away, but our rear guard advanced and attacked them right at the pickets. They were too late; just half an hour and they could have rubbed half of us out in the most favorable case before we could have gotten help. Everything went well, except the 30th Iowa Infantry lost its colonel and about 30 men wounded and 8 dead by advancing prematurely. They shot at the enemy before they noticed how strong they were and thereby received a battalion's salvo.[19]

The enemy was soon in full flight and General Osterhaus sent them 2 miles away with shells from two 20-pounder Parrots, which they feared not a little. Lieutenant W. Wangelin was hit between his thumb and pointer finger with a rifle ball. His fingers may remain stiff. His bones were not damaged. Another rifle ball went diagonally across his chest, went through his clothes to the skin, which it hardly touched. A third one stretched out his horse.[20] At 3 o'clock everything was over, and after we had eaten a hearty meal we finally lay down in bed and stayed there undisturbed until the following morning, asleep.

At 5 A.M. [October 22] out again. It was still raining. This is

---

[19] When Osterhaus received word from the commander of his cavalry picket that a large Rebel force pressed hard, he ordered his division to fall in. James A. Williamson advanced two battalions of his brigade and Woods's brigade took position to support either of his flanks. The two battalions pushed the enemy back to an open field; when the rest of Williamson's command came up and deployed, it met with a Rebel charge. Colonel William M. G. Torrence of the 30th Iowa lost his life before the enemy was driven back. Foiled in Osterhaus's front, Jeffrey Forrest's Rebels tried to cut into his left. Woods's regiments, part of the 12th Missouri included, took position to check the aborted attack. Osterhaus then dislodged the Confederates from their positions and drove them for five miles. The 30th Iowa's casualties were unrecorded but Osterhaus reported losing a total seven killed and twenty-eight wounded. *OR*, vol. 31, pt. 1, 17–18.

[20] Wangelin served as a member of Osterhaus's staff. Muster rolls, William Wangelin service record, NA.

carried out every morning as the enemy is pretty impudent, but will unlearn that under General Osterhaus's direction. This day was so cold and rainy that neither Southern gentlemen nor ourselves betrayed any great joy in chasing people; it passed uneventfully.

But next morning [October 23] it was clear (that is, *still* pitch dark) when at 2 o'clock we suddenly heard R-r-run, giff, gaff, hurry, hurry, hurry-fall in, fall in and the long roll, a fatal sleep destroyer. But we obey very fast and in a few minutes we stood "ready for action." But we didn't move out because it was just an enemy patrol of about 30–40 men who ran into our pickets and were warmly received. This morning [October 24] in the daylight, we found 4 horses, 5 rifles and about 12 hats that they must have completely forgotten in their haste to burn out of there. The horses were healthy and looking for their masters. They took the oath of allegiance and are now serving in the Union Army. On our side, nobody suffered any damage. At 6:00, our brigade moved out and marched over 4 miles, finding nothing but a few enemy pickets who tore off exceedingly fast. We went back, taking all pigs, etc. and usable furnishings with us. I don't know if we'll be visited again tomorrow.

Again, we are all hale and hearty. And I feel as lively or as quiet as I ever was, but fit as a fiddle. My heartiest and friendliest greetings to everybody,

from your true godson Henry

The daily harassment by Forrest's cavalry impeded somewhat the 15th Corps' advance toward Chattanooga, but logistical problems hobbled more effectively Sherman's campaign-toughened soldiers. He was under orders to repair the Memphis and Charleston railroad as he advanced, a time-consuming operation even under ideal conditions. Grant took overall command of Union forces in the West on October 19. After inspecting the Army of the Cumberland's perilous condition in Chattanooga, he untied his subordinate. Grant's order to forget the railroad and hasten eastward reached Sherman at Iuka on October 27, the day after he had set in motion plans to overcome the next great obstacle in his path, the Tennessee River.[21]

Sherman had planned an adroit maneuver to cover his crossing from the Rebel cavalry that hovered around his front like flies. Osterhaus's and Morgan L. Smith's divisions, under Frank P. Blair, drove toward Tuscumbia to keep Stephen D. Lee's Rebel cavalry busy while Sherman's other two divisions headed north to the river. Leaving camp at 3 A.M. on October 26,

---

[21] J. F. C. Fuller, *The Generalship of Ulysses S. Grant* (New York, 1929), 162, 166–67.

Osterhaus contacted the enemy six miles out on the Tuscumbia road. With Smith's division acting as a reserve, Osterhaus deployed his units and advanced across the rolling terrain to the Confederate position. Kircher and the 12th Missouri "advanced gallantly" on the right as skirmishers. As the captain succinctly reported, the Rebels "gave way on all sides."

Forrest made another, weaker effort on the other side of Caney Creek to hold, but Osterhaus drove him on, skirmishing most of the way. By evening, the two forces arrived within two miles of Tuscumbia and Forrest turned to do battle for a third time. He led a charge on Osterhaus's right, which the 3d Missouri shot into oblivion, wounding Forrest himself. The positions of the contending forces remained undisturbed as night and Blair's orders put an end to the fighting. Kircher's regiment had been skirmishing all day in the advance, struggling through the brush and muddy terrain. "We remained here[,] being worn out."[22]

October 27 emerged quiet and peaceful. Kircher could clearly see the Rebels move about in the same positions they had held the evening before. Osterhaus had orders from Blair to postpone his attack until Smith could flank the enemy on the Union left. Activity on the Rebel left prompted Osterhaus into action before Smith accomplished his task. Union artillery opened fire and skirmishers moved out, forcing back their gray counterparts. Soon, the whole Rebel command gave up its position and fled toward Tuscumbia, "a grand skadadle," as Kircher joyfully put it. By 11 A.M., Federal troops had possession of the place. They found Forrest lying in a house, shot through both hips. "A pleasent located town," Kircher thought, "had formerly about 1500 inhabitants but at present scarcely counts 200." The troops spent the night in its shelter.[23]

On October 28, in "pleasant weather," the two divisions marched sixteen miles back to their former camps without molestation from the battered Rebels. When they arrived at 4 P.M., they "were greeted by a full an[d] piercing tooting of the iron horse, which had made his way here during our 3 days tramp[;] he was wellcomed by many a hearty hurrah by our boys. It is in fact astounishing to see how fast the track, bridges and all is put in order by the engineer corps." Fatigued by his jaunt to Tuscumbia, Kircher longed only for "a sound sleep and a good supper. the supper soon was ready and the sleep followed."[24]

The Rebel horsemen could not leave Kircher alone. They followed Osterhaus from Tuscumbia and continued their harassment on October 29.

---

[22] *OR*, vol. 31, pt. 1, 19–21. Diary, Oct. 26, 1863.

[23] *OR*, vol. 31, pt. 1, 21. Diary, Oct. 27, 1863.

[24] Diary, Oct. 28, 1863. In a letter to his mother dated Nov. 2, 1863, Kircher reported that the Federals lost three or four killed and six or seven wounded in the fighting that led to Tuscumbia's fall. The Rebels, according to his estimate, lost thirty to forty dead and injured. Osterhaus did not report Rebel strength or losses but referred to his own casualties as "very slight." *OR*, vol. 31, pt. 1, 21.

"Up and to have my company in fighting trim was the work of but few minutes." The 3d and 12th Missouri positioned themselves to catch the enemy while the other Federal units pulled slowly back to draw the Confederates into a trap. As Osterhaus put it, he was "unable to entice the rebels within range." Kircher's men returned to their camp where the captain learned they were to "march in morning."[25]

Osterhaus's maneuvers of October 29 marked the true close of the Tuscumbia Expedition, which was an eminently successful operation. It enabled two 15th Corps divisions to cross the Tennessee at Chickasaw; Osterhaus's and Smith's divisions left their camps near Cherokee Station on October 30 to follow them. Smith went first, before the supply wagons, and Osterhaus marched behind the train. Federal cavalry covered his rear, which consisted of the 12th Missouri, 13th Illinois, and Landgraeber's battery.

Kircher was ready to go at 6 A.M., but his regiment had to wait four hours while the other troops scrambled over the rough roads. "It commenced to rain in all variations, thick, fine, cold and every discription. We had hardly marched 3 miles, when we had to stand in rain. . . . When turning round I was not at all surprised to see our cavalry about ½ mile off drawen up in line of battle and exchanging shots now and then with the rebs. The infantry marched into posish to be ready for the enemy should he feel very anxious to get whiped out. But he seemed to considre it very gravely, and was alas sattisfied to be left alone." With the wagon train stuck fast in the mud, the 12th Missouri marched a few hundred yards farther and bivouacked. "Fence rails were plenty and fires soon dried our wet clothing and made us somewhat more comfortable. But there was still something wanting—a supper. most men had some coffee with them and soon brewed some. Alas hurrah for Dan, he came with coffee, ham and hardbread. Smoking and sleeping now followed and we felt as gay as Kings (supposing they were in the same fix as we are)."[26]

The next day witnessed more of the same spasmodic marching. "About 11½ [A.M.] we began to move by jerks, every once in awhile marching 1000–2000 yards and laying down again. . . . The roads must be very bad ahead, or the 2nd divis. very poor in marching." At sundown, the 12th, 17th and 31st Missouri, with the 13th Illinois, camped three miles from Chickasaw. They were to stay as an outpost while the other regiments went on to the Tennessee. Federal cavalry captured a messenger headed for Rebel Gen. Philip D. Roddey, with instructions to capture the Yankee supply train. The only enemy disturbance occurred at midnight when 20–30 Confederates fired into the regimental camps and fled before Union picket fire.[27]

November 1 proved to be a day of tedious waiting. The 12th Missouri

---

[25] Diary, Oct. 29, 1863. *OR*, vol. 31, pt. 1, 22.

[26] Diary, Oct. 30, 1863.

[27] Diary, Oct. 31, 1863.

regimental officers' mess, of which Kircher was in charge, looked "very consumptive" to the young captain. "Our last crackers are eaten and last Coffee goes tomorrow." He hoped other regiments might arrive to relieve those at the outpost, which would enable him to replenish his stock when the 12th Missouri marched to the division camp at Chickasaw. No relief arrived. On the morning of November 2, the mess ate "jayhawked . . . beaf stake" before replacement units made their appearance. The 12th Missouri quickly made its way north and pitched camp on the Tennessee's south bank.

Kircher wasted no time in securing provisions for his officers. He also tended to necessary paperwork: a muster roll for Company E and a letter "to dear mother." "I hear G. Osterhaus is going to St. Louis," he wrote home, "as he is supposed to have gotten a dispatch that his wife was very sick. Col. Wangelin thinks dead. Whether I can give him the letter to take along I still don't know. Probably, we will go up the right side of the Tennessee tomorrow already, to—Chattanooga? Only the dear Lord knows."[28]

The work of crossing Osterhaus's division occupied the next two days. Three tranports, guarded by the gunboat *Lexington*, shuttled the regiments across. By 5 P.M. of November 3, all of Woods's brigade was over except the 12th Missouri and 13th Illinois. Kircher made ready to go, but Woods ordered the two regiments to stay and protect the 2d Brigade's crossing. "Old Zolz," as Kircher called Woods, "must have a pick at our or the 13th Ills. for we had to do dirty work for some time now." Woods assumed temporary command of the division when Osterhaus left that night to visit his dying wife. Kircher did not look with confidence on the change. "Old Zolz will make us all go to sleep or drink whiskey (provided we can get it). . . . I wonder how we will get along when in mess!"[29]

Woods finally allowed the Missouri and Illinois units to cross at 4 A.M., November 4. Kircher rested his men at Waterloo, on the Tennessee's north bank, until noon, when they joined the other troops in their eastward trek. The next day, rain descended to create "poor marching" and "wet dirty and hungry" men. On November 6, the division passed through Florence, Alabama, while the sun shone brightly.[30]

That night, Woods turned his command northward for a detour into southern Tennessee. Following the path of Smith's 2d Division, Kircher noticed signs of better times among the inhabitants. "[P]oltry and domestique animals are plenty." The citizens of Pulaski seemed well disposed in their relations with the blue-coated soldiers. "In fact it must be that Tennessee is beginning fast to be loyal again; farmers are mostly at home and attains to their business."

---

[28] Diary, Nov. 1, 2, 1863. Henry Kircher to mother, Nov. 2, 1863.
[29] Diary, Nov. 2, 3, 1863.
[30] Diary, Nov. 4–7, 1863.

The wagon trains slowed the infantry and provided extra duty for those soldiers who were assigned as escorts. On November 7, Kircher's men were among those distributed along the train, some of the "dirty work" Kircher thought Woods delegated too often to the 12th Missouri. On November 9, Kircher was late in stopping for the night because he had to follow the wagons. Frustration vented itself in irritability. "It was quite dark, teams had been in some time but still the dam niggers had made no motion toward pitching our tent, the cook had not commenced supper yet and to crown all, [Captain Charles H.] Kibler A.A.G. of Old Zolz had plaied us a trick and ordered our teams in a swampy cornfield. The infernal Q.M. also gave us no meat, and all meat jayhawked on march was confiscated so we had something extra Spec[ial,] Crackers and Coffee. All were in a very good mood to thrash any one who crossed his path."[31]

On Kircher's birthday, November 10, the head of Woods's division closed up on Smith's rear and halted for the remainder of the day. The unexpected rest felt good to Kircher, as he enjoyed the chicken his officers' mess cook had found. Yet, campaigning through Civil War Tennessee was not easy. "I wounder how mother spend her birthday. I hope not as troublesome as I."[32]

The hard marching continued. On November 11, Kircher passed through Fayetteville, Tennessee. The next day, Woods's division marched closer toward Alabama, heading south. "Instead of hill, rocks and clear Creakes with sandy bottoms, the road runs through mar[s]hy Post Oak timber[.] we hardly pass any farms. . . . our wagons hardly got through the mire today, the dead mules and horses strewen along the roadside prove the hard work they had gon through."[33]

Kircher crossed the state line on November 13, his brigade again bringing up the 15th Corps rear. He marched through New Market, "a small settlement, looks pretty much plaied out." There, he "noticed some 15 or 20 women young and old standin partially in a house or porch and a yelling, houling and fussing worse [than a] collection of darkies at a camp meeting, and the cause of all these grimmazes was the death of an old man. Men must be scarce in the south now a days."[34]

Light began to appear at the end of the tunnel as Woods's division passed Maysville on November 14 and went on to camp near the Memphis and Charleston Railroad. His semicircular detour completed, Kircher could look forward to a more direct line of march to Chattanooga. That night, he "plaied a trick on Old Zolz, snatching a calf from his cook." Kircher's small victory did not change the regiment's marching position. He again walked in

---

[31] Diary, Nov. 7, 9, 1863.
[32] Diary, Nov. 10, 1863.
[33] Diary, Nov. 11, 12, 1863.
[34] Diary, Nov. 13, 1863.

the rear guard on November 15, camping at Larkinsville. The division reached Bellefonte near the Tennessee River the next day. "Found no citizens at all here," Kircher reported, "all houses are vancant. looks dreary."[35]

Stevenson, Alabama, provided little better scenery. "The whole town consists of about 10–15 houses," Kircher noted when he entered it on November 17, "quite small potatoe." After tramping so long across rough country, the soldiers were ready for more exciting fare than that found on the march. "There was a general rush for the sutler shops, which were in great numbers, and all pretty well striped of everything." Kircher hoped to rest and "take a general wash" at Stevenson the next day, but higher authorities pushed Woods's division on to Bridgeport. It arrived early in the afternoon and Kircher finally found time to write his mother.[36]

> Camp near North Bank Tennessee River
> at Bridgeport Ala. November 18th 1863

Dear Mother!

Before I talk about anything else, I want to give you a short outline of the pleasures that we have experienced in the last 14 days. You know about us until the 4th from my letter of the [second], that I sent from Chickasaw with General Osterhaus's orderly (I didn't want to bother the General himself, as such a sad dispatch had been sent to him). From Bert, I hear that the General arrived just early enough to accompany his wife to her cold grave. It is a very hard blow for him and all the poor children. But everybody's hour will strike, soon or late. Man proposes, God disposes.

So, on the 4th at 3 A.M., we set out marching with the rest of the division across the river about 2 miles to Waterloo and camped until 11:00. We broke up again and marched day in and day out until 2 P.M. today, when we got here. On an average, we went 15–16 miles a day: in all, close to 200 miles in 14 days.

The various cities and villages, or rather hamlets, that we passed were : Chickasaw, Waterloo, Gravelly Springs, Florence, Lexington, [Alabama]; XPulaski, XFayetteville, [Tennessee]; New Market, XLarkinsville, XBellefonte, and XStevenson [Alabama]. The towns with an X are railroad stations, and until 3 years ago, with the exception of Stevenson, were probably quite busy, nice little towns of 1000–1500 inhabitants. But now there are few people there and many houses stand empty or are burned down. Of the others, only Florence is more than 15–25 houses strong. But the

[35] Diary, Nov. 14–16, 1863.
[36] Diary, Nov. 17–18, 1863.

latter may have been a quite prosperous town of 2–3000. I just went through it on the march and just a small part, but I noticed a large building a la knight's castle with rooms, etc. As I heard, this had been an institution to turn young fireeaters into chivalrous Southern gentlemen, what we would probably call a "College" in this country.

Not far from there was a second large building, more a la temple, surrounded and decorated by a mass of pillars; whether Roman, Greek or Southern chivalrous style I don't know. Except I learned that it was to train Southern teenage girls to be belles or ladies; in other words, to perfect their rocking in the rocking chair. I had to laugh at our boys because just as we were marching past this remarkable temple there came a governess or some kind of shriveled lovely tripping out, and rang her little bell quite angrily. But the young girls who want to become ladies took more interest in us, and didn't hear until the jingling got quite dreadful. And our boys almost made the unfortunate partners-in-suffering belonging to Miss "Whatsername" gloomy with "hurrahs for breakfast." I wonder if there might have been a shower of slaps and of tears.

But I am getting way off the track. On the whole march we didn't see a single enemy. The gorillas (guerrillas) don't serve as well when it gets cold and the leaves are off the trees.

The region is really, really very beautiful in places. But for a farmer it is not an Illinois by far. It is remarkable that where the ground doesn't consist chiefly of gravel and sand in the valleys the way is boggy and marshy, so that our pioneers always had to spend a lot of time before our trains were able to pass. By the way, without any sense or reason, we took the longest and the worst route. Just look on the map. We went in a zigzag.[37] Now we are finally here and survived everything; praise and thanks be to God that a human can stand much more than a mule or a packhorse. This is evidenced by the many wounded quadrupeds that adorn the route on both sides and that make it highly unpleasant for our noses.

Nobody knows what is to become of us. I can just tell you this much; that we are going across the Tennessee near Bridgeport (the railroad is working that far)[38] tomorrow or the next day, where the

---

[37] Sherman ordered the "zigzag" march into southern Tennesse to effect a more convenient crossing of Elk River, at Fayetteville. A southerly crossing would have required ferrying or bridge building; both were time-consuming projects. *OR*, vol. 31, pt. 2, 571.

[38] The Memphis and Charleston Railroad had not been completed from Cherokee Station to Bridgeport; that construction had been postponed when the 15th Corps left Cherokee to

4th, 3d, and 2d divisions of the 15th A. Corps are already assembled, about 30,000 men, besides 2 divisions of [Joseph] Hooker's, as I hear. All the time you hear first this then that, and then both of those are again tossed into a cocked hat by a third story.

However, I do believe this much; that the next 14 days will bring us a great step nearer to the end of the war and probably bring happiness to many by giving them eternal peace, unhappiness to many by making cripples out of them. And the loved ones who are far from them but are present in their thoughts must console themselves with the knowledge that they too have done their honest part for freedom, for the preservation of their country. The harder it seems to them, the more certainly they know that they have paid their obligation.

We are all well and trusty and are looking forward to tomorow as it *might* be a day of rest. Bert played stupid today. A wagon wheel ran over his right foot and pinched it. It hurts, nothing more.

Your loyal and sincere son Henry

Following his trek across northern Alabama and through southern Tennessee, Kircher rested at Bridgeport all day on the nineteenth. On the twentieth, he was up and out again. The 12th Missouri crossed the Tennessee on a pontoon bridge that connected a long island, almost in the river's center, with both banks. The Nashville Railroad was restored on both sides and army engineers were fast at work on a bridge to arch over the stream. "A fine rain" fell all afternoon and night, and continued the next morning when Kircher marched to Shell Mound.[39]

On the morning of the twenty-second, he moved still closer to the goal of that lengthy campaign begun exactly two months before. With battle more imminent as he stepped off each mile, Kircher wished Osterhaus was back in the field. "We dont feel safe with old Holtz [another nickname for Woods], although he carefully avoids to come in range or contact of any guns or contents thereof." The "very picturesque and romantic" countryside contrasted sharply with roads that were "awful rocky, muddy[,] full of holes and almost insurpassable for waggons." He camped that evening at Whiteside Station.

At noon that day, Osterhaus reappeared from his sad errand home. His German soldiers encouraged his return while the American-born Woods returned to a brigade command. "A smile and thundering cheers burst frome

---

march northward across the Tennessee. The railroad that ran to Bridgeport from Nashville had been put into operation as a supply line.

[39] Diary, Nov. 19–21, 1863.

Brig. Gen. Peter J. Osterhaus.

all [Osterhaus's] division (except the 76 Ohio but they are small potatoes, and no one notices there doing.) and we again feel like Uncle Sam's boys ought to[,] 'sure of victory.' "[40]

Kircher's unit left the Whiteside Station camp at midnight, November 22. At 2 P.M. the next day, Osterhaus's division arrived below the northwest face of Lookout Mountain, atop which lay Bragg's left flank.[41] The rest of the Confederate army was positioned atop Missionary Ridge, to the east, stretching northward to the Tennessee River above Chattanooga. As the

[40] Diary, Nov. 22, 1863. The 76th Ohio was Woods's old regiment. Like a German unit in a predominantly American outfit, it suffered because of ethnic chauvinism.
[41] Diary, Nov. 23, 1863.

15th Corps came up, it crossed the river on a pontoon bridge below town. Grant's battle plan called for its march upstream and crossing the river again to assault the Rebel right on Missionary Ridge.

Confederate efforts to harass Federal movements cut off the last 15th Corps division. The Rebels shoved trees into the river, which floated down and damaged the bridge before Osterhaus's men marched to the north side. Rather than wait for repairs, Sherman "left one of [his] best divisions" on the south side in Lookout's shadow, while he moved up the river as planned. Osterhaus was attached to Joseph Hooker's command. Leading an ad hoc collection of three divisions from three different armies, Hooker prepared to assault and capture the mountain. Meanwhile, closer to Chattanooga, George H. Thomas's Army of the Cumberland took possession of Orchard Knob in preparation for the coming fight. Kircher heard the gunfire, on the other side of Lookout, but could not see the action.[42]

He joined the grand battle on November 24, faithfully recording it in diary entries that ably summarized the strife. "At six all troops were put in motion and marched to their different points for attack on west side of Lookout Mt. it was very foggy all morning so that we hardly could see any of the upper part of the Mountain. It was to our advantage, because the enemy

---

[42] *OR*, vol. 31, pt. 2, 572. Diary, Nov. 23, 1863.

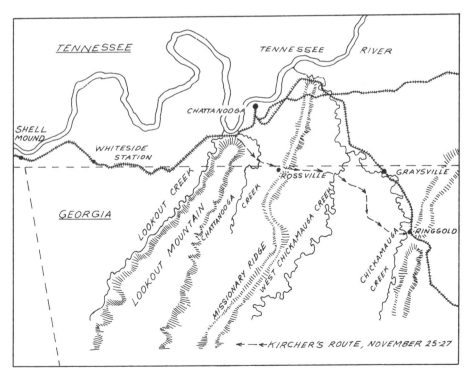

Chattanooga, Ringgold, and vicinity

could not see our movements. about 10 first cannon shot was fired, our side commenced. we our division was in second line. advanced up the mount and swept along the whole side half way up and around to east side of the mount where the rebs are in force yet. First line advanced to the rock crown of the mount, when the darkness put a stop to advancements, but firing was Kept up untill 11 at night. A great many deserters came to us as we advanced, some two or 5[,] as some say[,] pieces of artilry was taken on the hill by first line, and about 2000 prisoners and deserters lay all night at yesterday's last posish."

November 25: "At 6½ A.M. first cannon shots to disturb the peace that rained all over since midnight, were fired on our extreme left some 7–8 miles. At 6.30 minutes a thundering hurrah from the very crest of Loockout mountain notified us of the rebels skedadle during the night. About 11 our division and the 12 A.C. under Genral Hookers command marched along east side of Lookout M. to Missionary ridge, had to make the bridge across [Chattanooga] creek first. Although in the meanwhile the infantry of our division crossed and flanked the rebel left at [Rossville] gap[,] where road passes through ridge. when arrived there after a good deal of Klimbing Mountain they had skedadled. we followed in double quick and got in to the rear of the rebel left[.] this made them breake and run in confusion. took some 900 prisoners and 1 piece of artillery. night now closes all fun, and safed the rebs from a more thourough routing[,] if it could be more so.

"Marched to the rebel fighting ground on Missionary Ridge and bevouacked. Here one thundering hurrah after the other burst forth frome the 12th Army C. and our division as Genr. Hoocker approched. Still prisoners are brought in, in squads of 3 to 12. they all look healthy and gay and many of them have but little more fight in them, think their cause a lost one[;] so do I, and besides I hope thourough punishment awaits them. Here an occasional shot to left and front very distant, suppose it to be near Jhonson Station.

"So the day closed, and yet our regiment had but 2–3 lightly wounded[.] but tired we were, and although only my Great coat accompanied me I managed to get some rest during the night, it was rather cold."

That day, Bragg's grip on Chattanooga was broken. Sherman's assaults on the northern end of Missionary Ridge proved to be futile, but Thomas's frontal attack and Hooker's envelopment of Bragg's left sent the Rebels flying southeastward. On November 26, Hooker pursued.

"This morning I hear our division alone had taken about 1000 prisoners since yesterday morning and about 1000 stand of armes, one 12 pdr Howitzer and 2–3 Colors[;] quite a deaseant grab for one day's fun. Marched about 10½ a.m. to the Johnson road and proceeded our march thereon for some 5–6 miles. had to make four large bridges across the checkamauga creek, which had been destroyed by the rebs on their retreat. the road[,] wich had been good untill now, turned to be very muddy and swampy[.] made but slow progress and camped about midnight[.] Our (Officers not men) rations give out to day, I am somewhat in trouble now being member of committee, but unforeseen things can't be helpt."

Hooker continued his pursuit on November 27, coming across Bragg's rear guard stationed in a gap just east of Ringgold, Georgia, twenty miles southeast of Chattanooga. His artillery was far to the rear, struggling across rough roads, and the Rebels, Patrick Cleburne's division of tough fighters, held very strong defensive positions. Hooker rashly ordered frontal assaults, hoping enemy resistance would prove to be as susceptible to Yankee power as it had been on the twenty-fourth and twenty-fifth.

Because it was in the vanguard, Osterhaus's division bore the brunt of proving Hooker wrong. The German positioned his 3d, 12th and 31st Missouri to form a solid center behind the railroad embankment, and sent regiments to the left and right to attack or harass Cleburne's defenders. In fighting that lasted most of the morning, all assaults by Osterhaus's and other divisions were repulsed.

At one point, Osterhaus sent part of the 12th Missouri forward to reinforce 17th Missouri skirmishers who, in conjunction with soldiers of the 13th Illinois, converged fire on a Rebel battery in the gap. Annoyed, some of Cleburne's regiments charged, driving the skirmishers back on the main line behind the railroad. There they were halted by well-directed fire, but it proved to be weak revenge for the blunt failures of all Federal attacks that day. By noon, the Rebel general realized that Bragg's army was at a safe distance. He pulled out of the gap, leaving Hooker with almost 500 casualties.[43]

With Cleburne gone and the Rebel army far away, Osterhaus's men took stock of their losses. Ringgold was a vicious, worthless fight, completely overshadowed by the great victories on Lookout Mountain and Missionary Ridge. Dead leaves, grass, and bushes on the ridge slopes had caught fire, suffocating many of the wounded and scorching dead bodies.[44] Osterhaus pointed out in his official report "the very heavy percentage of losses among" his officers, while "expressing the highest praise for their energy, valor, and, in fact, every virtue which honors a good soldier." Woods noted that the 12th Missouri, "although exposed to a severe fire, held its position with undaunted courage." A rumor circulated after the battle that the regiment lost almost its entire staff of officers when two Rebel units tricked it into an ambush.[45]

The rumor proved to be untrue, but the reality was bad enough. The 12th Missouri lost six officers and twenty-one enlisted men. Henry Kircher was one of those who fell before that "severe fire." A Rebel rifle ball plunged

---

[43] *OR*, vol. 31, pt. 2, 323, 604–5, 608.

[44] Andrew G. Henderson to wife and children, Mar. 29, 1864, A. G. Henderson Papers, Iowa State Historical Department, Division of Historical Museum and Archives, Des Moines.

[45] *OR*, vol. 31, pt. 2, 71, 605, 608.

into his right arm, shattering the bone. He fell and was sitting on the ground when a second ball smashed into his left leg. It split the tibia wide enough for a finger to be inserted into the fracture. Helping hands carried the defense-less captain away, but a third ball struck him in transit, causing a flesh-wound.[46] When he listed names of those whose actions seemed worthy of mention, Woods included "Capt. H. A. Kircher." Pairing him with an officer of the 27th Missouri, the brigade leader noted they had "received their wounds while gallantly doing their duty." Ringgold convinced Grant to call off Hooker's pursuit, and the urgent task of caring for the wounded was begun.[47]

---

[46] Muster rolls, Compiled Service Records: casualty sheet, undated, Henry Kircher service record, NA.

[47] *OR*, vol. 31, pt. 2, 322–23, 609.

CHAPTER EIGHT

"A Young Man, and Popular"

Surgeon Joseph Spiegelhalter worked hard following the Ringgold fight. He gave personal and expert attention to Kircher's injuries when the still-conscious captain was carried to a house near the battlefield. There, Spiegelhalter noticed his arm and leg wounds bled freely. He quickly examined Kircher and ordered him moved immediately to a back room, where a fire burned for warmth and light, and a table stood ready for work.

Spiegelhalter recorded the ensuing moments in terse detail. "The Capt. took it very easy & told me that I would have to cut off his arm. Informed him that I was going to put him under the influence of chloroform in order to examine his wounds closely & that I had as much fear for his leg, as for his arm; at the same time I asked his permission to amputate his leg also, if it should be necessary. This he gave me, by telling me to do whatever I thought best."[1]

Anesthetized by the chloroform, Kircher did not feel the probings of Spiegelhalter or two associates the doctor called for consultation. Assistant Surgeon Frederick Hohly of the 12th Missouri and Assistant Surgeon Charles Bruckner of the 17th Missouri examined the wounds and agreed that amputation was necessary. Spiegelhalter performed the double operation. He removed Kircher's right arm six inches below the shoulder and severed his left leg "between the middle and lower third." The surgeon noted that Kircher withstood the surgery with relatively little loss of blood. After the stumps were dressed and the patient bedded comfortably, his appearance seemed "very encouraging" to Spiegelhalter.[2]

As soon as Kircher awoke and felt sufficiently strong, he recorded in agonized penmanship the list of friends and comrades shot down before the fatal gap. A rifle ball had shattered Hugo Wangelin's right elbow joint when he had raised his arm to give directions to the regiment. That same day, surgeons cut off the useless limb. Lt. Col. Jacob Kaercher, despite a slight wound, had taken command of the 12th Missouri. Capt. Joseph Ledergerber had been shot through the lungs and spine, and had died later that day. His

---

[1] Casualty sheet, undated, Henry Kircher service record, NA. Spiegelhalter wrote this narrative in his letterbook. He loaned it to the War Department sometime later, perhaps in relation to Kircher's pension, and relevant passages were copied onto a casualty sheet for inclusion in the captain's service record.

[2] Ibid. Medical certificate, Aug. 13, 1864, Engelmann-Kircher Collection.

brother, Maj. Fred Tell Ledergerber, had received a leg wound. Kircher did not fail to note his own injuries with startling objectivity: "left leg and right arm amputated about the upper joints[,] therefore this smearing."[3]

Belleville received news of the casualties on November 28 when a dispatch from Osterhaus arrived. "The late battles near Chattanooga have put our county into mourning," proclaimed the editors of the *Advocate*. They also reported that Henry Goedeking, Frederick K. Ropiequet, and Bernhard Wick left town on November 29 to help care for the "brave sufferers." The three men reached Chattanooga less than a week later.[4]

By the time his godfather met him, Kircher had already made progress toward recovery. His sometimes cryptic diary entries record the struggle. November 28: "after passing a sleepless night we were put in an old RR. Car and some men shoved it toward Chattanooga. about dark we found out that a bridge ahead was burned and we had to turn back 2 miles to Grayville were we lay all night. it was awfull cold. some of the wounded had but 1 blanket and suffered greatly."

On November 29, Kircher "passed a hard day." Horse-drawn ambulances arrived after dark to transport the wounded past the burned bridge. After spending one more night in the cars, Kircher left on November 30. "This morning early we were all packed in ambulances and drove toward Chattanooga about 12 miles. I had to suffer a great deal from the roughness of the road. just sundown I arrived at Chatt. and was put in tent with Col and Maj in Field hospital of A[rmy] of [the] C[umberland]."

The Cumberlanders took care of Kircher, but he felt lost without his old unit. His December 1 entry, "get along slowly[,] treatment non[e] at all[,] leg pains," does not show it. But on December 2, he wrote with heartfelt gratitude: "alas our division arr[i]ved and our Doctors are here[;] god bless them they are noble sols."

Among his own people again, Kircher left the hospital and on December 3 was taken to a house where he found accommodations more comfortable. By the fifth he could write "my stomps geat along well." That evening, Goedeking, Ropiequet, and Wick found him. The day before, as soon as he had reached Chattanooga, Goedeking had reassured Augusta of her son's safety. "Much loss of blood," he had telegraphed, "but is doing well." He had discovered that the wounded were scheduled to leave for their homes in three weeks. Wick and Ropiequet left for Belleville on the evening of December 6, but Goedeking stayed with his wounded friend. He kept in touch with Joseph through the mail.[5]

---

[3] Muster rolls; casualty sheets, undated, Hugo Wangelin, Jacob Kaercher, Joseph and Fred Tell Ledergerber service records, NA. Diary, Nov. 27, 1863.

[4] *Belleville Advocate*, Dec. 4, 1863.

[5] Goedeking's telegram to Augusta was erroneously dated Dec. 7.

Chattanooga Dec. 7, 1863

Dear Kircher!

I can add little to what Wick and Ropiequet will report. Heinrich looks pale, since he lost a lot of blood from his arm. Dr. Spiegelhalter has told me in the meantime that, unless unforseen circumstances occur, the healing is going unexpectedly well and that he can proceed with me, Wangelin and Ledergerber on the 20th of December.

It is very bad that my condition is not capable of giving even the slightest bit of help. I can't bend over or move and am therefore very upset.[6]

You can imagine that it is a pleasure for me to come to you with Heinrich. I hope that you have had weather in plentiful supply like here. The weather is magnificent here.

Heinrich wants to add something, which will probably be the dearest part to you. Your wife will have received the telegraphic dispatches. Greet her heartily from me. A nigger is coming along anyhow, a nice mulatto who takes care of Heinrich. I am in agreement with that, for he will be quite necessary, as Heinrich requires much care and lifting.

Your Heinrich Goedeking

Just to let you see that my writing has not been impeded completely. Things are going as well as one can desire under such circumstances. In 3 weeks, we will probably see each other again. Many greetings to everybody.

Your faithful Henry

Kircher's recovery proceeded well, as Spiegelhalter had informed Goedeking. On December 8, he was "getting along fast, only have pains some times, but appetite all the time." Two days later, he felt "tired laying in bed, have go[o]d deal of pains at times." Casimir Andel visited the wounded with gifts of fruit on a "rainy, muddy and cold" December 12 and Kircher thought on the fifteenth "about starting north with first opportunity."[7]

In Belleville, Joseph's thoughts embraced his son and he expressed them in a letter.

Belleville Decbr 14, 1863

My dear Heinrich!

The report from Wick that you are as well as can be expected,

---

6 See Joseph's Dec. 14 letter to Henry for an explanation.

7 Diary, Dec. 8, 10, 12, 15, 1863.

under the circumstances, and are fighting energetically and success-
fully against depression was very reassuring to us. The loss of the
leg and the arm is hard, but there remains nothing else to do but to
adjust to what cannot be changed and to fit yourself into anything
that will clearly lead to alleviate it. It must always be a great comfort to us that it occurred for our country, which deserved to be re-
membered all the time.

Wick's report that the amputation of the leg succeeded very
well was reassuring, since that will increase the usefulness of the
artificial leg so that in time you can walk without a crutch and cane.
In a year, you will be able to write just as well with the left hand as
you were able to do; and as you know, it is rare that somebody
amasses a fortune by working with his hands. It is chiefly one's
head, intellectual work, that brings it to light. In time, you will find
the suitable activity in which you can gain a considerable fortune by
thrift and industry.

We heard from Wick, with great regret, that Goedeking fell
over a trestlework and hurt himself. It disturbed us very much, although Wick reported to us that the doctor told him it was nothing, just that it would take him a few weeks to get over the pain.

Ropiequet, who is staying in Lebanon, has letters from you
and Goedeking, I hear. We all, and especially Mother, are glad that
you wrote a few lines. Wick speaks with great praise of your manly
spirit and brave attitude.

Now you are probably in Bridgeport at Osterhaus's for better
care of the patients. And, as Wick says, on the 20th you will begin
the journey home. Your room is all ready.

The most cordial, best and heartiest greetings from us all to
you and Goedeking.

Your loving Father

Joseph erred in believing Kircher had alrady traveled to Bridgeport. As
Albert Affleck informed him on the thirteenth, the wounded remained
when Osterhaus's division left Chattanooga for that place on December 4.
Affleck heard that Kircher was "in good spirits, and his wounds healing
rapidly."[8]

As time passed, it became clear to his father that Kircher's misfortune
was felt by many. From faraway Springfield, Missouri, the site of Henry's
first exposure to the human aftermath of battle, came a consolatory letter

---

[8] Albert Affleck to Joseph Kircher, Dec. 13, 1863.

addressed to Joseph. Charles Stierlin, a Belleville marble sculptor and Kircher family acquaintance, expressed feelings shared by all of Henry's friends.[9]

                             Camp near Springfield Mo. Dec. 7th 1863

Mr. Jos. Kircher Belleville Ills.

Honored Sir!

After I completed my chief work on December 4, I took the Missouri *Democrat* of December 2 in my hands in my tent. Right on the first page the headline "Killed and wounded in the 12th Missouri" struck my eyes. I quickly skimmed the few lines. I could hardly trust my eyes when it said at the end: "Capt. Kircher wounded in arm and leg amputated." The unfortunate paper fell involuntarily out of my hands. I couldn't believe it and had to read it again, but the *Westliche Post* of December 1 removed all doubt.

It is true that, since exactly one year ago today at the Battle of Prairie Grove and ever since, I have seen many a brave comrade fall beside me. But after the loss of my dear brother Wienand, a captain in the 22nd Illinois, whereby my good old mother in Germany lost her youngest son and favorite in this war and besides separated by the wide ocean, no case has touched me so painfully as this sorrowful news. I could not neglect expressing to you, the deeply grieved father of such a brave son, my deeply felt, sincere sympathy over this hard blow.

I know that Heinrich is the pride and joy of his parents, and rightfully so, and I know with what tenderness his brothers and sisters cling to him. I have become acquainted with the magnificent trait of his spotless character, and therefore am able to appreciate the pain that this misfortune has caused in the family. No glowing iron could sear so painfully in the heart of the tender mother of such a son as the news of this blow! On a fine fall day in 1861, I saw the 12th Missouri regiment pull out of St. Louis full of courage and fire—then it was in Concordia Park and our battery in Fort No. 3. I saw Heinrich, Wangelin and other young Bellevillers give me a friendly farewell. At that time, I thought what a great sacrifice it is for the parents of *such* sons to offer them to their Fatherland.

Won't his mother's heart accompany Heinrich in all his difficulties? Won't she raise up Schiller's words of prophecy every evening: "Dies Kind, kein Engel ist so rein,/ Lasst's Eurer Huld emp-

---

[9] *Belleville Advocate*, Nov. 23, 1859.

fohlen sein!" [This child, no angel is so pure,/May it be commended to your favor.] I had hoped to see Heinrich grown to be a blooming youth full of potential after a long absence. And now, crippled like a young oak! It would be a useless undertaking for me to try to console the family about this misfortune, the pain is too much. If anything could cool the burning wounds, it would have to be the knowledge of the overall feeling of pain that the news gave to everybody who knows him. Virgil's "Solamen miseris socios habuisse malorum" is in this case a poor comfort!

It is true that there is almost no family left in America that hasn't suffered from the loss of one of its members. But I believe I may boldly say that no family had more or more justified hopes for its favorite, and none gave the Fatherland a greater sacrifice than Heinrich's kin. He is justifiably both loved and respected by both Germans and Americans. Of course, it is a proud knowledge for everyone who has participated in this struggle against the greatest curse of this century, and history will record forever the names of all the heroes of this holy cause in this way to a grateful posterity. But will the pain of the parents also be honored, who buckled on their favorite's sword so full of hope and well, and then receive him back in such a condition? Hardly! For the deeply grieved parents, there remains only the awareness that they have done their part in the achievement of the noble end result of this war.

In hopes that this goal may soon be reached and that Heinrich's wounds do not turn out to be so unfortunate that they can't soon be healed, and that patience and strength enough remain for him to have a speedy recovery; that namely Providence will keep the parents' and brothers' and sisters' courage up in their pain and they will not succumb to it, I sign with sincere sympathy and respect.

Charles Stierlin 1st Lieut.
Comdg. Battery "L"
1st Mo. Light Artillery

Kircher began his final journey home on December 19, aided by Goedeking and Louis. The party left Chattanooga aboard the steamer *Dunbar* and traveled to Bridgeport, where Kircher stayed in Osterhaus's private tent while waiting for the paperwork of his sick leave to be completed. On December 21, Osterhaus set his worn division on the road to Woodville, Alabama, to spend the winter. It was a sad day, the last time Kircher saw the unit with which he had endured so much. As it headed west, Kircher boarded the train and started north at 5 P.M.

The rail trip proceeded smoothly to Nashville, where Kircher waited four hours before continuing to Louisville. From that place, on the twenty-third he rode in a carriage across the Ohio to New Albany, Indiana. Kircher continued by rail but was delayed twelve hours on December 24 by an accident on another part of the line. When traffic resumed its normal pace, he came nearer and nearer to home. The train reached O'Fallon at 10 P.M. Christmas Eve, and Kircher found his father "patiently waiting" there since the day before. At 2 A.M., Christmas morning, he arrived home, "amongs parents brother and sisters." For Kircher, the battles and campaigns had ended.[10]

He remained a captain in the 12th Missouri on sick leave for the duration of his enlistment term. The paperwork for such an arrangement was handled by willing friends. In the field, Albert Affleck took care of the necessary records for Company E until a replacement could be appointed for Kircher.[11] In St. Louis, Surgeon Spiegelhalter worked hard to thread the bureaucratic needles for his former patient's benefit. Spiegelhalter had accompanied a group of wounded soldiers north and tried to do all he could before returning to the field.

St. Louis, Mo. January 4th, 186[4]

Dear Henry!

Enclosed, you receive your account to sign. I had the pleasure of meeting Mr. Paymaster in a very good mood; he found the "Papers all correct," and told me to come back this afternoon to pick up the account.

You need to sign the same and send along a certificate from a notary public on a special piece of paper. The paymaster, Major Ballard, will then send you a check on the U.S. Treasury or pay the money to somebody authorized by you (for example, Mr. Bremermann). It would be best for you to write him a few lines and tell him in what manner you wish to receive your money. The notary public must attest that he knows you and that this is your signature.

I am glad that you can now get your money without further ado. The only other thing that could still cause you some trouble is the money for Responsibility of arms, etc. I hear that people are having quite a bit of difficulty getting it here. Anyway, I will do my best this afternoon. Today, I will not get away from here but tomorrow I *must* in any case.

Your Jos. Spiegelhalter

---

[10] Diary, Dec. 19–25, 1863.
[11] Albert Affleck to Henry Kircher, Feb. 24, 1864.

Arrangements for his financial security were settled until the late summer of 1864. Kircher's handicap added even more urgency to the important question of a postwar career for the soon-to-be civilian. With the greatness of a heart big enough to sacrifice for a friend, Henry Goedeking answered the question. He offered to help Kircher break into local politics. County elections for the office of Circuit Court Clerk were scheduled for November, 1864, and Goedeking announced his candidacy in late March. He published a unique plea in the local newspaper, explaining that he ran not on his own but on Kircher's behalf. "I shall, if elected," he declared, "superintend the office with him, so that his youth, and inexperience need create no apprehension. He shall however have the emoluments of the office, even if his corporal disability shall prevent him from attending to the duties of the same." If there was a note of paternalism in the proposed arrangement there was also love and gratitude for a citizen who had gallantly endured adversity. "For his benefit," Goedeking continued, "I hope to receive the cordial support of the voters of our county, who can thereby show their acknowledgement of the merits of a soldier wounded and crippled in their cause."[12]

Kircher whole-heartedly endorsed Goedeking's unselfish act. "My youth, my inexperience, and my almost helpless condition, would render me unable to attend to the duties of an office requiring such labor; neither could I make myelf personally acquainted with my constituents throughout the county; hence I am induced to accept the offer of my kind and generous friend."[13] His election campaign played further on the image of a worthy soldier who had sacrificed much for the cause. A photograph depicting Kircher in uniform, balancing himself with one arm and leg, was made and distributed.

While the political juices simmered, Kircher had plenty of time to think about the war. Although far to the south, it was ever ready to intrude into his Belleville life. The wastage of Ringgold still haunted the town's citizens and they found assurance of the worth of their cause in Joseph Ledergerber's funeral. The body of Kircher's fellow officer was brought home for burial on April 9. It lay in state at the Courthouse, attended by the Belleville City Guards, and was laid to rest in the Ledergerber family plot outside town on the eleventh.

Fred Tell Ledergerber, home on leave to recuperate from his Ringgold wound, listened as an old family friend pronounced the eulogy. Lawyer Jehu Baker recounted Joseph's life and military career, and summed up the cause of the war as "the diabolic spirit of slavery." Like the citizens who had gathered at the Courthouse almost exactly three years before, Baker saw the conflict as a simple opposition of good and evil: "Slavery against Demo-

---

[12] *Belleville Advocate,* Apr. 22, 1864.
[13] Ibid.

Capt. Henry A. Kircher's political campaign photograph, 1864.

cracy! The meanest Despotism against the purest Liberty!" The struggle's momentous importance added meaning to the sacrifice and the sacrifice inspired further effort for the cause. "I know of [no] occasion more fitting," Baker proclaimed, "than the funerals of heroes to awaken just sentiments of public duty in the minds of living men." Family friends were so pleased with the eulogy that they asked Baker to publish it in the local press. The "kindness and respect" shown Joseph by everyone so touched Fred Tell that he offered "the thanks of a soldier who has lost a brother and a comrade" to the citizens of Belleville. Soon after the funeral, he was off again to the war.[14]

After so many months of faithful service with the 12th Missouri, Kircher could only watch from a distance as the old regiment unfolded the last pages of its history. The winter months of 1864 passed easily for the unit in its camp at Woodville. Wangelin returned to the field on March 15 to take charge of the regiment's brigade, while Kaercher continued to lead the 12th Missouri.[15]

The campaign for Atlanta began in May and the regiment participated in nearly the entire operation. Other than skirmishes, however, it fought only three pitched battles. At Resaca, on May 14, it conspicuously captured an important bridge across Camp Creek and boldly held it as a forward position in the face of enemy fire. As a reward, the regiment was one of the first to march into Resaca when the town fell. Near Dallas, on May 27 and 28, the 12th Missouri helped to repel vicious Rebel assaults on Osterhaus's division.[16]

Regimental losses ran high and claimed more of Kircher's friends. William Bechtel was shot through the right side of his chest on May 27. The wound proved to be fatal; he died on June 5 at New Hope Church. Fifty-three other regimenters were counted among the casualties of Sherman's long campaign for the strategic gate city of the South.[17] As Jacob Kaercher wrote to Missouri's adjutant general in June, "the 12th is now but the sceleton of a regiment, and if it suffers as severely during the battles yet to be fought, as it has in every engagement heretofore, I fear the Relatives and friends of the 'Boys' will have but few to welcome home in August or September next."[18]

Albert Affleck's letters arrived, keeping Kircher appraised of the regiment's condition. He wrote of the wounded, the dead, citing figures and naming names. He wrote of the rain that beat on shelterless soldiers, the "very poor eating," the marching and digging of trenches, the marching again and the progress of Sherman's careful and relentless drive south. At Roswell, they destroyed factories and captured factory girls, "a gay sight," and continued the campaign.[19]

---

[14] Ibid., Apr. 15, 22, 1864.
[15] Muster rolls, Hugo Wangelin and Jacob Kaercher service records, NA.
[16] *OR*, vol. 38, pt. 3, 126–27, 129–31, 164.
[17] Muster rolls, Compiled Service Records: casualty sheets, undated, William Bechtel service record, NA.
[18] Jacob Kaercher to Adj. Gen. John B. Gray, June 7, 1864, Miscellaneous Papers, Adjutant General's Office, Jefferson City, Missouri.
[19] Albert Affleck to Henry Kircher, May 20, June 8, July 16, 1864.

Kircher sent copies of his campaign photograph to Affleck in July. "I am well pleased with the pictures," Bert responded; "of course I should prefer to see the other limbs, but that you know is impossible." To his closest friend, Affleck could be frank. The long months of service wore heavily on him and he thought often of going home. "Dear Old (Pal)," he wrote, "in one month my time will be out, and I expect to be in Belleville about the first of September[;] will we not have a big time then? I shall be glad to get home as soon as possible after this Campaign is over, for I feel worn out and tired[.] I need rest and good living for a time, and then I shall be ready to go into service again if I am needed."[20]

The powerful war intruded again, to smash Affleck's plans and make of his homecoming a macabre contrast to the "big time" he had expected. The 12th Missouri participated in one more battle before its muster out, at Ezra Church, on July 28. The Rebel army made savage frontal assaults on Sherman's men, who fought behind hastily improvised breastworks. The regiment was in the thick of it and helped to repulse the attacks by the sheer weight of Confederate losses.[21]

Casualties in the Federal army were comparatively light but they included Jacob Kaercher. Wounded severely in the chest, he nevertheless survived. Albert Affleck was not so fortunate. For the third time in the war he was injured in combat. He battled leg and abdomen wounds for several days, struggling to overcome this final obstacle to a safe return to home and friends. On August 4, nine days before his term of service expired, he died in the field.[22]

Conflicting rumors concerning his fate reached Belleville for more than a week after. Some stories claimed that he had survived his wounds with the loss of a leg, while others reported his demise. His distressed father left for Georgia to seek the truth. By August 19, confirmation of Affleck's death appeared in the newspapers. His body reached Belleville on August 24 and the citizens crowded once again to pay respects to one of their young men killed in war. The remains lay in state at the Courthouse and were interred on August 25.[23]

Affleck's death, more than any other, touched Kircher deeply. He had had to watch helplessly as the old regimenters fought on, and now his closest comrade was added to those already gone. Affleck's last letter to Kircher was written on July 26 and contained a report of Sherman's victory in the Battle of Atlanta four days before. On its reverse side, Kircher noted in still wobbly penmanship that Bert had been shot through both thighs at Ezra Church and had died after suffering terribly. He had been only twenty-four, two

---

[20] Ibid., July 16, 1864.

[21] *OR*, vol. 38, pt. 3, 167–68.

[22] Casualty sheets, undated, Jacob Kaercher and Albert Affleck service records, NA.

[23] *Belleville Advocate*, Aug. 12, 19, 1864. *Belleville Democrat*, Aug. 27, 1864.

years older than Kircher himself. "So one by one all my friends are droping off to live in a better world than this, O Will we ever mete again?"[24]

The regiment came home, not in a group as it had left St. Louis three years before, but in fragments. Companies A, B, and D reached St. Louis on August 12. Mayor James Thomas and the Veteran Reception Committee paraded them through the city and treated the men to speeches. Adj. Gen. John B. Gray thanked the veterans on behalf of the citizens of both Missouri and Illinois. After partaking of refreshments at Washington Hall, they marched to Benton Barracks for muster out.[25]

Companies A and B received a second welcome when they returned to Belleville on August 21. Majin's Band, the Illinois and St. Clair Fire Companies, and numerous citizens offered them lunch served at the City Park.[26] Inevitably, speeches followed. Colonel Nathan Niles, formerly of the 130th Illinois Infantry, tried to sum up the motives of his fellow soldiers in going to war. "You know what you have been fighting for. . . . You know the blessings of Union, the evils of disunion, the good of a single nationality, and the curse of anarchy." He recounted the many campaigns and the sad attrition of officers. "One, it is true, is here at his home, Capt. Henry Kircher, but his right arm and left leg he has left behind in Georgia." With their work done, Niles urged the veterans to live up to the reputation society gave them. "Let your deportment as citizens and civilians be worthy of you and your great deeds as defenders of your country. . . . Let your future be worthy of that glorious record which you have written for yourselves, a record which is a part of your country's history."[27] When Company E mustered out on September 3, Kircher's term of service ended. After more than three years and four months, he was once again a civilian.[28]

The fall election swung heavily in his favor. A newspaper correspondent described him as "a young man, and popular." Union men supported his candidacy,[29] but he remained largely independent in political doctrine.[30] The race for Circuit Clerk was not even close. Kircher won 4,316 votes to his opponent's 2,643.[31] On March 20, 1865, he began his four-year term of of-

[24] Albert Affleck to Henry Kircher, July 26, 1864. An ironic accident occurred in the Affleck household the same week Albert died. A three-inch shell, found near the family residence and stored in the kitchen for several weeks, exploded from the heat of the stove, which it destroyed. The explosion slightly injured one of Albert's brothers and seriously burned a servant. The family thought the projectlle was a solid shot and did not expect it to explode. *Belleville Advocate*, Aug. 12, 1864.

[25] *St. Louis Daily Missouri Democrat*, Aug. 13, 1864.

[26] *Belleville Advocate*, Aug. 25, 1864.

[27] Ibid., Sept. 2, 1864.

[28] Muster rolls, Compiled Service Records: Muster rolls, Henry Kircher service record, NA.

[29] *Belleville Advocate*, Oct. 28, 1864.

[30] Newton Bateman, ed., *Historical Encyclopedia of Illinois and History of St. Clair County*, vol. 2 (Chicago, 1907) 1054.

[31] *Belleville Advocate*, Nov. 18, 1864.

fice. Only six months later, the man responsible for his new position left him; Henry Goedeking died on September 28 after a brief illness.[32] Kircher quite early was on his own. He creditably performed his duties and left the Court in 1869 to take Goedeking's place in the hardware firm. The business changed its name to Kircher and Son and truly became a family affair.[33]

As Clerk, Kircher obtained a unique opportunity to form an acquaintance with his former commander. A popular hero following the war's end, William T. Sherman addressed a letter to the Recorder of St. Clair County in September, 1865, requesting a deed transcript for a forty-acre farm he had bought near Caseyville thirteen years earlier. Kircher promptly complied and became involved in aiding Sherman with his business deals. The general wanted either to sell the farm or enlarge it. Because of a low offer, he decided to keep the forty acres and buy more land adjacent to it. His agent had neglected to pay the taxes while Sherman was fighting in the South, and he understood that soldiers received special consideration in such matters because of their absence. "If such be the case, surely I was absent at the War."

The general and the ex-sergeant exchanged several letters during the course of their business acquaintance. The relationship possessed the possibility of developing on a personal level, but Kircher could lay no claim to membership in Sherman's circle. The two arranged for a meeting in 1865 to discuss business regarding the farm and Sherman expressed pleasure at knowing that Kircher's fellow citizens had rewarded him with a responsible civic position. Considering Kircher's bitter remarks about Sherman at Chickasaw Bluffs and the May 22 assault at Vicksburg, it was ironic that the general consistently signed himself "Your friend."[34]

By the time Kircher joined his father's store as a partner, the major themes of his life had been set: the sense of duty to his country, expressed in his Civil War service; the sense of civic responsibility, expressed in his clerkship for the Circuit Court; his strong devotion to family cohesiveness, which was consummated in the firm of Kircher and Son. The young man built a career for himself in a variety of business ventures, such as banking, utilities, and hardware production.[35] Reinforcing his ethnic heritage, he became an officer of the Belleville Printing Company, which published a German-language newspaper entitled *Der Stern*. The first issue came off the press on October 28, 1877, and the paper ran for several years.[36]

His career as a public servant dovetailed with his business life. He became active in the Board of Education and the Kindergarten Association,

[32] Ibid., Mar. 17, Oct. 6, 1865.

[33] Bateman, ed., *Historical Encyclopedia, Illinois, St. Clair*, 2:1054.

[34] William T. Sherman to County Recorder, Sept. 19, 1865; Sherman to Henry Kircher, Sept. 22, Dec. 30, 1865.

[35] *Belleville Advocate*, Jan. 12, Feb. 9, 1872; Apr. 6, 1888.

[36] *History of St. Clair County, Illinois* (1881; reprint, Marissa, Ill., 1975), 108.

and reentered local politics.[37] Elected mayor of Belleville in 1877 in a four-way race that netted him more than twice the number of votes received by his closest competitor, he served two one-year terms.[38] His most conspicuous public service occurred in July 1877, when he took action to guard life and property during a strike of railroad employees.[39]

Kircher's missing limbs did not prevent him from realizing his dream of travel. In 1871, he went to Germany to visit Joseph's family at Fulda and stayed in Europe a short time in 1872.[40] The war wounds also failed to keep from him another avenue of personal fulfillment—marriage. For his bride, he chose Bertha Engelmann, a member of one of St. Clair County's most substantial German-American families. Her father knew the Kirchers well and the impending wedding pleased everyone.[41]

Kircher immersed himself in preparing his new home, Pine Grove, for Bertha. As he told her in a letter, the place required much work. Of his surviving letters, this is the nearest to a love missive. Its confident pensmanship and pleasant subject matter contrast with his diary entries following the Battle of Ringgold, a symbol of Kircher's personal conquest of the war's legacy to him.

Pine Grove Apl 18-80

My dear Bertha!

As a reward, despite the hot, oppressive weather, I permit myself to bore you a little with a short letter. You have arrived home in good shape and have found everybody well and healthy. Your father, on account of the rainy weather, was certainly also present and enjoyed loving his Bertha once more.

You will ask in what way am I diligent. I have sent you a list of porcelain and given instructions that your order should be followed exactly and well. However, for some errors you too will have to suffer. Then, I have helped my Sunday carpenter to raise the grape arbor. We have changed the shelves in the basement in such a way that the passage to the wine cellar about which you complained will be mostly free.

I fixed all manner of things in the garden while Dick enjoyed the fresh grass. This afternoon I have until now, 4.30 P.M., swept piles that were just mixed up with each other and arranged things to suit myself. I have been fixing decorations for the ceiling of your

[37] *Belleville Advocate*, Apr. 11, 1873; Dec. 25, 1874.
[38] Ibid., Apr. 20, 1877. *History of St. Clair County*, 188.
[39] *Belleville Advocate*, July 27, 1877.
[40] Two diaries, written in German in 1871 and 1872, describe Kircher's European travels.
[41] Theodore Engelmann to Joseph Kircher, Apr. 19, 1880.

little room and I hope you will enjoy it. Also, there are your roses, which specifically grew for you in a round flower bed across from your northeast window.

Today is really a day of spring and it seems you can see things grow. I have asked Ed to help with the windows in the renovated part [of the house]. So now, this is done and in the meantime you have closed your shutters, for it is a south, southeast wind. And now that we are done, there are not only black clouds but a thunderstorm. Charles Hilgard and wife wanted to visit you and asked me yesterday if it would rain, which I predicted. But it shouldn't keep him from visiting you and maybe it wouldn't rain.

It starts to get dark and this sheet is almost used up. There is so much that I wanted to do yet, or have done before you become my dear wife, so that you would find everything in good order. But 2 weeks will pass and I will be surprised if only half the work is done. And it will take another 2 long, long weeks. If I don't finish it, my dear Bertha has to have patience and even help me a little.

Until we go to St. Louis together, be greeted with all my heart from

your Henry

The ceremony took place on the Engelmann farm on May 1, 1880. Kircher's old army comrades were there to celebrate. Casimir Andel gave the couple silver breakfast forks and Fred Tell Ledergerber presented them a silver pickle dish. The more studious Surgeon Spiegelhalter, now a prominent St. Louis physician, presented the Kirchers with "an elegantly bound vol. of Wm. Tell, handsomely illustrated." The guests feasted on a lavish meal and the newlyweds boarded a train for St. Louis. They left that city the same evening for a honeymoon tour of the eastern states.[42]

During their sixteen-year marriage, the couple had three sons: Harry Bertram, Joseph Casimir, and Theodore Engelmann.[43] Bertha died at an early age, forty-seven, on January 2, 1896. Her passing occurred four years before the death of Kircher's mother at age eighty-nine. Joseph Kircher had died in May, 1888 and Henry had reincorporated the hardware firm of Kircher and Son in 1889, so that a new generation of the Kircher clan, in his three teen-aged sons, stood ready to continue the family tradition.[44] A solid business, the store that Joseph Kircher and Henry Goedeking had started in 1848 survived both war and the passing of its founders.

That Kircher transcended his disabilities is evidenced by his success in

[42] *Belleville Advocate*, May 7, 1880.
[43] Bateman, ed., *Historical Encyclopedia, Illinois, St. Clair*, 2:1054.
[44] *Belleville Advocate*, May 4, 1888; Feb. 15, 1889; Jan. 10, 1896; Jan. 5, 1900.

building a good life for his family and in the high example of his civic actions. But the missing limbs offered constant reminders of that fateful day outside Ringgold. In addition to his business enterprises and public service jobs, Kircher received a government pension for his wounds. He applied for it on September 24, 1864 and was awarded $20 per month. Periodic increases raised the payment to $50 by 1874 and $72 by 1889.[45] In the latter year, the higher rate was made retroactive to 1878.[46]

Even after Bertha's death, Henry continued to be active and productive in business, besides caring for his three sons. A simple cold finally accomplished what three wounds had not; the cold developed into pneumonia and Kircher died on May 1, 1908, at age sixty-six. His death "came as a distinct shock to his numerous friends and the people of Belleville in general," according to the town's newspaper, which printed a traditional obituary.[47] Machinist, soldier, circuit clerk, businessman, mayor, husband, and father; the few lines of such a résumé could not be more than an imperfect shadow of the man, written by a generation not alive to feel the pulse of events that witnessed Kircher's part in the crusade to save the Union.

In his quietly impressive way, Kircher had fulfilled the admonition of Colonel Niles when he welcomed the 12th Missouri veterans in 1864; his civilian life had proved to be as conscientious and successful as his Civil War service had been. Kircher possessed the will to endure and perpetuate; his family, his community, and in a larger sense his nation, were his beneficiaries.

---

[45] Pension application, Sept. 24, 1864, Henry Kircher Pension File, Records of the Adjutant General's Office, NA. The pension was made effective from Sept. 4, 1864. Pension certificate, July 29, 1889, Engelmann-Kircher Collection.
[46] *Belleville Advocate,* Nov. 8, 1889.
[47] Ibid., May 1, 1908.

Bibliographical Essay

Unpublished Sources

The most important source in the preparation of this book was Henry Kircher's Civil War letters and diaries in the Engelmann-Kircher Collection of the Illinois State Historical Library. His papers include some postwar correspondence and diaries. A medical certificate and a pension certificate also are pertinent to his war experiences. A few letters by Kircher's father and mother, written during the war years, and a postwar letter by Kircher's prospective father-in-law, Theodore Englemann, are filed among his papers. Henry Goedeking's letters, including one in English, also are included, as are seventeen letters by August Mersy of the 9th Illinois Infantry. Albert Affleck's war letters, written in English while he served in the 12th Missouri, and three letters by William T. Sherman can be found in the Kircher papers.

Kircher's Pension File in the Adjutant General's Office, National Archives, provided useful information on his postwar life. The National Archives also holds the military service records of all 12th Missourians. They have been microfilmed under the title Compiled Service Records of Volunteer Union Soldiers Who Served in Organizations from the State of Missouri, Rolls 487–95, Microcopy No. 405. When I used these compiled records as a single source, I gave a short citation of the above title. More often, I used the service records of individual soldiers. In both instances, the specific documents within the service records that were used also were cited. The Missouri Adjutant General's Office at Jefferson City holds the 12th Missouri Descriptive Roll. It also has a letter by regimental commander Jacob Kaercher in its Miscellaneous Papers. The Andrew G. Henderson Papers at the Iowa State Historical Department, Division of Historical Museum and Archives, includes a letter by Henderson that describes the Ringgold fight. He served in the 31st Iowa Infantry, which was part of James A. Williamson's 2d Brigade of Osterhaus's division.

Newspapers

The best source of information on Belleville, St. Clair County, and the citizens of both during the war years is the *Belleville Advocate*. Of much less importance but yielding some useful information is the *Belleville Democrat*. Research in both sources was greatly facilitated by the existence of a newspaper index compiled by WPA workers in the 1930s and housed in the Belleville Public Library. Correspondents' dispatches in the *Chicago Daily Tribune* and the *St. Louis Daily Missouri Democrat* provided useful background information.

Books

Secondary works pertinent to the history of Belleville and St. Clair County include Alvin Louis Nebelsick, *A History of Belleville* (1951; reprint, Belleville, 1978); *History of St. Clair County, Illinois* (1881; reprint, Marissa, Ill., 1975); Newton Bateman, et al., eds., *Historical Encyclopedia of Illinois and History of Evanston*, 2 vols. (Chicago, 1906); Newton Bateman, ed., *Historical Encyclopedia of Illinois and History of St. Clair County*, 2 vols. (Chicago, 1907). Joseph C. G. Kennedy, *Population of the United States in 1860; Compiled From the Original Returns of the Eighth Census* (Washington, D.C., 1864), provided useful information on the percentage of foreign-born residents of St. Clair County. On a wider geographic scale, Arthur C. Cole, *The Era of the Civil War, 1848–1870: The Centennial History of Illinois* (Springfield, 1919), was very useful for detailing state history during the war years.

Second in importance only to the Kircher papers in the preparation of this book was the *OR*, more formally known as *The War of the Rebellion: A Compilation of the Official Records of the Union and Confederate Armies*, 128 vols. (Washington, D.C., 1880–1902). Several other compilations served as valuable sources of information, including Frederick H. Dyer, *A Compendium of the War of the Rebellion*, 3 vols. (1908; reprint, New York, 1959); Francis B. Heitman, *Historical Register and Dictionary of the United States Army*, 2 vols. (1903; reprint, Urbana, 1965); *Report of the Adjutant General of the State of Illinois*, 9 vols. (Springfield, 1900–1902).

No books on the 12th Missouri or its sister units, the 3d and 17th Missouri, have been written. Histories of two other regiments offered only bits of information relevant to this work: *Military History and Reminiscences of the Thirteenth Regiment of Illinois Volunteer Infantry in the Civil War in the United States, 1861–1865* (Chicago, 1892), and Marian Morrison, *A History of the Ninth Regiment Illinois Volunteer Infantry* (Monmouth, Ill., 1864).

Secondary works of a more general scope provided useful background information. Edwin C. Bearss, *Decision in Mississippi* (Jackson, Miss., 1962), covers essentially Grant's Vicksburg campaign. Bruce Catton, *Grant Moves South* (Boston, 1960), is still the best military biography of Grant during the first two years of the war. J. F. C. Fuller, *The Generalship of Ulysses S. Grant* (New York, 1929), was useful on occasion, as was B. H. Liddell Hart, *Sherman: Soldier, Realist, American* (1929; reprint, New York, 1958). There is a real need for a new study of Sherman's personality and military career. Kircher reminds us that Sherman's generalship at places like Chickasaw Bluffs was much weaker than some of his biographers have conceded. Finally, Francis A. Lord, *They Fought For the Union* (Harrisburg, Pa., 1960), was useful for information on the mobilization of Union volunteers.

Articles

The only published work on Kircher's regiment is Earl J. Hess, "The 12th Missouri Infantry: A Socio-Military Profile of a Union Regiment," *Missouri Historical Review* 76, no. 1 (1981):53–77. In this article, I used some quotes from Kircher's letters to support narrative and analysis. A revealing diary quote relating to regimental discipline appears on p. 71 of the article. I did not, however, find a place for it in this book.

Two works that contribute biographical information on people mentioned here are Dumas Malone, ed., *Dictionary of American Biography,* 20 vols. (New York, 1928–36), and William G. Bek, "The Followers of Duden," *Missouri Historical Review* 16, no. 1 (1921):119–45. The former contains articles on Gustave Koerner, Peter J. Osterhaus, and Charles Rau; the latter includes lists of pupils at Frederick Steines's German-American school in Missouri before the war.

Richard S. West, Jr., "Gunboats in the Swamps: The Yazoo Pass Expedition," *Civil War History* 9, no. 2 (1963):157–66, provided helpful information on a unique campaign of the Civil War. Bearss's *Decision in Mississippi* also contains a full account of the Yazoo Pass Expedition.

Index

Earl J. Hess has taught at Southeast Missouri State University and is now pursuing his doctorate at Purdue University. He has published articles on the Civil War in *Civil War History, Missouri Historical Review, Georgia Historical Quarterly*, and *Lincoln Herald*.